CRUISING NORWAY
2019-20

Oslo to Kristiansund

CONTENTS
Volume 1

Introduction	2
Cruising Options for Norway	5
Geography of Norway	10
A Norwegian History	19
Oslo - The National Metropolis and Capital	25
Stavanger	49
Haugesund	63
Bergen - Norway's Second City	73
Sognefjord - Visiting Fläm and Gudvangen	94
Nordfjorden - Visiting Olden	108
Ålesund	119
Storfjorden - Visiting Hellesylt and Geiranger	133
Kristiansund	149
About the Author	165

The majority of maps used in this book are taken from Open Street Map contributors and are so noted for each map. For further information contact: *www.openstreetmap.com*

INTRODUCTION

A map of Norway and Svalbard

I have been cruising Norway for the past ten years, and have visited all of the major ports of call along its long and convoluted coastline, In 2017 I finally felt it was time to present a book on Cruising Norway. This volume is the first major revision, updating the material for the 2019 and 2020 cruise seasons. Of all the places in the world where the cruise industry has developed itineraries, none can compare with the raw natural landscapes of intense beauty combined with the romantic Viking history that are found in Norway, one of the most sought after travel destinations for those who love to travel by ship. The major cruise lines with their mega liners can only visit the most important ports of call in Norway while the more upmarket or adventure oriented cruise lines operating smaller ships provide more comprehensive itineraries capable of including small ports of call that are not able to accommodate the large sea going vessels.

This title, which now comes in two volumes provides you with an overview of Norway of its physical characteristics and challenging geography and a moderately detailed history to enable you to best appreciate the country without having to delve into complex academic treatises on either subject. Often my readers ask me to add more minute geographic or historic detail, but with the size limit Amazon sets for a book, to satisfy the wishes of so many readers I have now created this update in a two volume set. Volume 1 starts with a basic introduction to Norway and cruising its waters. It then takes you from Oslo in the south to Kristiansund in the middle coast where most one-week cruises turn around and start back. Volume 2 continues the journey north of Kristiansund starting with Trondheim and taking you to North Cape. There is also a supplement on Murmansk and Archangelsk in Russia for those of you fortunate enough to add these Arctic ports to your itinerary.

The aim of this two-volume set is to enable you to gain a sufficient understanding of the physical and cultural landscapes of Norway along with a look at the country's history to then focus upon the enjoyment of the ports of call your cruise includes, not to be able to pass a college exam on the subject.

I have included all of the ports of call visited by both the major cruise lines and the upmarket and adventure cruise companies. I have left out those very minor ports that can only be visited utilizing the local ferry boats or combined mail/passenger services that ply the hundreds of small fjords and bays, connecting nearly every village with the rest of the country. This book gives the reader the essentials on the ports that are likely to be a part of the itineraries of the majority of cruise lines.

I trust you will find this book both informative and sufficiently enticing to whet your appetite for a cruise along the coast and through the fjords of Norway.

Dr. Lew Deitch,
February 2019

Early morning calm in Storfjorden

A bright and sunny day in Geirangerfjorden

CRUISING OPTIONS FOR NORWAY

Most of the major cruise lines offer summertime Norwegian Fjord itineraries. These cruise lines vary in price and of course in the levels of quality service and cuisine being offered. The itineraries vary from short one-week cruises to two weeks or longer. I strongly recommend cruise itineraries that are devoted only to the Norwegian ports and that begin and terminate either in Copenhagen or Oslo. In this way you are not spending days at sea between such starting or ending ports as Southampton, Edinburgh or Amsterdam. Why spend time at sea that could be better spent in Norway. You must choose your cruise line and the itinerary carefully to maximize how much of the country you will see, recognizing that Norway is so vast that you cannot get more than an introduction to its land and people on a single cruise even if it is two weeks in length. After ten years of cruising Norway, there are still a handful of ports capable of hosting a the smaller more adventure oriented cruise ships that I have not visited.

Your choice of cruise line must be guided by the following factors to maximize your enjoyment:

* The amount of time you wish to spend on the cruise. The longer the time frame, the more ports of call and fjords you can visit. With the majority of cruises starting in Oslo, Copenhagen or Bergen, a minimum of two weeks is needed to explore well north into the Arctic region of Norway, a portion of the country that should not be missed because it offers a hauntingly magnificent landscape.

* The level of luxury and the number of on board amenities are important factors to many who cruise, often of equal value as the itinerary itself. The most luxurious ships are primarily found in the fleets of Silversea, Seaborne and Regent. These ships are relatively small and can offer more detailed itineraries that include ports seldom if ever visited by the larger cruise ships. The higher end cruise lines offer staterooms that are generally larger and better appointed than the mega ships belonging to the major mass market companies. There is also a higher ratio of crewmembers to passengers, thus giving more personalized and attentive service. Likewise the cuisine on the smaller up market lines is gourmet oriented, and often provides a taste of the countries being visited. But because these ships are smaller and carry fewer passengers their theaters and casinos are likewise not overly large and the entertainment is not as lavish. One must choose between having a more sedate and elegant atmosphere or "glitz" and glamour of the larger vessels.

* The level of detail that you wish to experience is a guiding factor. For the most intensive exposure to the more remote locations in Norway, there are a few adventure cruise ships that will offer itineraries that visit the most inaccessible ports or fjords that are not visited by either large or luxury cruise ships. Also Norway's Hurtigruten line offers the most extensive itineraries on its local mail runs and adventure oriented cruise ships. They also offer cruises during the winter months, a time when the majority of travelers are looking at tropical itineraries. Although the days are exceptionally short or even nonexistent above the Arctic Circle, the major attraction is the dramatic beauty of the Aurora Borealis or Northern Lights.

For those who are new to cruising or who have not traveled to Norway, here are some basic tips that will help to maximize your voyage:

* Always book an outside cabin if traveling on one of the larger ships that offer less expensive interior cabins, which have neither a window nor a veranda. Interior cabins can be quite claustrophobic because it is always necessary to use artificial illumination. At night these cabins are totally dark to where a nightlight is needed in the event you want to get out of bed for any reason. And without at least a window, you will miss so much of the local scenery in transit between ports of call. Much of the joy in cruising Norway is to just sit and soak in the passing scenery. Remember that daylight hours are extensive during the spring and summer months and much of the time you are close to the shore, traveling the inside passages or within the fjords.

* To economize, book an outside cabin with a window, as these are generally on the lower passenger decks where a veranda is not provided. One advantage in rough seas is that being lower down in the ship equals more stability when the ship begins to pitch or roll. There are often rough waters in the North Sea, especially on the transit between the northern tip of Denmark and the southern coast of Norway. And generally the weather is not conducive to wanting to sit outside on a verandah.

* Although forward lower deck cabins are offered at the lowest prices, be aware that the ship's maneuvering thrusters and anchors are forward. You will be exposed to a fair amount of noise when the ship is entering or leaving a harbor, rotating its position prior to docking and during docking maneuvers, and this can often interrupt your morning sleep, especially if you tend to be a light sleeper.

* If having the opportunity to enjoy fresh air at any time is important to you, then it is wise to book a cabin with a veranda even though you will not spend much time sitting out of doors. While traveling in Norway there is often so much scenery to be enjoyed from your cabin while in transit between ports.

* Whenever possible book a cabin in mid ship, as when a ship begins to pitch the mid-section acts like the fulcrum in that it experiences far less movement than either forward or aft cabins. The North Sea is noted for squalls that can cause the sea to become choppy. Once inside the fjords, the seas are generally exceptionally calm. But during transits between fjords or while en route from or returning to either Oslo or Copenhagen you may find that the conditions can be quite uncomfortable. I have seen waves of ten meters in the waters between Bergen and Copenhagen.

* If you should become queasy during periods of rough weather and pitching or rolling sea, it is best to go up on deck or out on your verandah and breath some fresh air. Also by staring off at the horizon the body surprisingly is less stressed by motion. But if you are unable to go out on deck because of the danger presented during really inclement weather, it is still possible to sit near a window and from time to time look out to sea, toward the horizon. Fear also plays a role in the way you feel during rough seas. If you become frightened that the ship may capsize or sink, it will only heighten your feeling of uneasiness. Remember that ships can take a lot of punishment, and it is rare for a modern cruise liner to go down in rough weather. Starving one's self when feeling queasy will only make the condition worse. Dry

crackers or toast along with hot tea is one way to calm an irritated stomach. And there are patches, pills or injections available from the ship's medical office to calm extreme discomfort.

* Be prepared for sudden changes in the weather. During summertime, the average temperatures in Norway are in the teens or very low 20's Celsius, which is between 50 and 75 degrees Fahrenheit. Occasional summer rainstorms can drop temperatures and it is easy to become chilled or soaked if not properly dressed or carrying an umbrella. Dressing in layers is the best way to accommodate the changes that can occur on a given day. And yes there are occasional hot, humid days when the sky is blue, the sun feels strong and temperatures can climb up to between 25 and 30 degrees Celsius, which is between 77 and 86 degrees Fahrenheit, but these are the exception rather than the rule.

* Do not over indulge in eating or drinking. It is best to pace yourself and try and eat normally, as you would at home. Overindulgence only leads to discomfort and added weight gain. And even though meals are included on board ship, one of the delights is in having a meal ashore. Norway is noted for its fresh fish and seafood. And Norwegian cuisine is elegantly prepared and one of the delights of the country.

* When in port, weigh the option of going on organized tours against freelancing and visiting on your own. If you have any sense of adventure, a local map, public transit information and the names of basic venues make it possible to see as much, if not more, in a relaxed atmosphere in contract to being shepherded around as part of a tour group. Also by striking off on your own you have more opportunity to mingle with and meet local residents. And in Norway most people do speak English as their second language, with many also speaking German. But in some of the more remote locations or smaller villages the only option is to take organized tours offered by your cruise line, as local tour operators, taxis or busses are few in number.

* When starting a cruise, arrive at least 24 hours ahead of the departure and spend a minimum of one night in the port of embarkation. This enables you to recover from jet lag and to become acclimated to a new environment.

* When disembarking, it is also recommended that you spend at least one night in the final port of call before flying home. Two nights are preferable if your port of departure is either Copenhagen or Oslo.

* When on shore in Norway it is safe to eat without fear of gastrointestinal upset. The country maintains a high degree of sanitation, and good restaurants abound. And drinking the local water is totally safe even though most restaurants offer bottled water.

* Violent crime in Norway is rare. The ports of call on the itineraries are exceptionally safe. However, pickpockets are found almost everywhere in the major cities such as Copenhagen, Oslo, Bergen and Trondheim where tourists will be seen in greater numbers. So wise precautions always apply regarding not keeping a wallet in a back pocket, not showing large sums of money and for women to keep a tight rein on their handbags.

* The use of credit cards is widespread at all major restaurants and shops. However, in Europe data chips are the norm. If your credit card has a data chip, insert it into the front of the credit card machine and follow the prompts. You will either enter a pin code or wait for the receipt to be issued and then sign it. Cards without a data chip will require a special pin code. Check with your credit card service before leaving.

* In Norway the national currency is the Norwegian Kroner. The use of the Euro, Pound or other foreign currency is rare, and only the occasional tourist oriented shop may be willing to accept other currencies. It is best to obtain Norwegian Kroner at an ATM or currency exchange at the start of your cruise. The easiest option is to order it in advance from your personal bank at home before departing.

* Returning to the ship is normally expedited by having your cruise identification card handy to be swiped by the security officers. Packages and large handbags are often put through an x-ray machine similar to what is used at airports. And passengers pass through an arch to screen for any major metal objects.

* Most ships offer hand sanitizers at the gangway and recommend that you sanitize your hands upon return. This is not mandatory, but it never hurts to be cautious. Norway is one of the cleanest countries in the world, but still a bit of extra precaution is a good policy.

The Norwegian Kroner comes in the following denominations of graduated sizes and there are coins for values below 50 Kroner

GEOGRAPHY OF NORWAY

The topography of Norway with its coastline of fjords and offshore islands. (Maps of Europe, Creative Commons Attribution Share Alike 3.0 license)

Norway is the westernmost nation of the Scandinavian Peninsula with its southern coast on the Kattegat and Skagerrak, a waterway that is actually an extension of the North Sea. However, historically Norway, Denmark and Sweden have been interwoven throughout time and even today there are close bonds between the three nations that consider themselves to be the heartland of Scandinavia. Iceland is also geographically a part of Scandinavia, but it is located almost midway between mainland Europe and Greenland, yet culturally it is a European nation. Finland, which was occupied by Sweden during much of its early history, is also considered to be a Scandinavian nation, however, linguistically Finnish is not a Germanic language, as are Swedish, Norwegian, Danish and Icelandic.

Geographically Norway is considered to be an elongated nation, essentially meaning that its shape has one axis that is far greater than the other. In this case, the north to south distance across Norway averages nearly 1,800 kilometers or 1,100 miles while its east to west extent in the south is less than 200 kilometers or 120 miles. In the far north there are locations where the country is less than 100 kilometers or 60 miles in width. Given its highly indented coastline and nearly 50,000 offshore islands, the total Norwegian coastline is nearly 22,000 kilometers or 13,620 miles in length.

The total land area of Norway covers 323,802 square kilometers or 125,000 square miles, which is approximately the size of the American state of New Mexico. But it is the elongated shape that makes the country appear to be so much larger than its total land area indicates. Norway extends over 13 degrees of latitude, extending north to just over 71 degrees North Latitude, making it the most northerly location in all of Europe. Approximately one third of the length of Norway extends north of the Arctic Circle, giving this region 24 hours of total daylight for nearly two months and then a reversal in winter with 24 hours of total darkness. In actuality, all of Norway experiences long summer days and long winter nights.

Norway's total population is only 5,207,689 (as estimated in 2015 by the CIA World Factbook). Over 1,000,000 live in the greater Oslo region.

THE NORWEGIAN LANDSCAPE: Norway is essentially a mountainous country, one of the most rugged countries in Europe with over 70 percent of the country consisting of mountain slopes. Only 2.7 percent of the country is considered to be arable, yet the Norwegians are able to develop pastures and orchards along with small garden plots on slopes that seem to be impossible to access. This is also a nation in which over 2/3 of the land is raw wilderness, so steep or so far north and cold that it has not been settled. And the combination of high altitude and high latitude, especially north of the Arctic Circle also means that much of the land is above the tree line, and sits bare and windswept. Once you are north of the Arctic Circle you will find that without snow cover during summer the land almost resembles a desert region because of its lack of significant vegetation. Geographers call these far northern lands polar deserts and you will understand why when you visit.

The Scandinavian Mountains serve as the backbone or spine of the nation with spurs extending both east and west from the central ridges. The highest peak reaches an elevation of 2,469 meters or 8,100 feet above sea level. The median elevation of the land is just over 460 meters or 1,500 feet. These are old mountains that share a common thread with the mountains of the British Isles and the Appalachians of North America. It is believed that they once were part of the ancient continent of Pangaea prior to its breaking apart to slowly form the continents we know today. These mountains were heavily glaciated during the Ice Age or Pleistocene, as much of the land was buried under more than a kilometer of ice. As the ice advanced and retreated four times over several million years, it sculpted and gouged, deepening former river valleys along with grinding down and sharpening many of the highest peaks. The landscapes of Norway are among the most spectacular and beautiful of any nation. This is a country of superlatives. The Scandinavian Mountains extend the entire length of the nation and are broken by deep valleys that once carried glaciers down to the sea during the four great glacial advances. In the far north, there are still many small active glaciers to this day. As the glacial ice sculpted these deep valleys, they were turned from "V" shape river valleys into wide "U" shape gashes through the scour and pressure exerted by the moving ice. Very steep nearly vertical walls leading up to the higher peaks are the hallmarks of glacially created valleys. As the sea level rose with the last glacial retreat, many of the high mountaintops were left standing as islands while these deeply carved valleys flooded with seawater to form the magnificent Norwegian fjords. Thus present-day Norway has a coastline that is over 22,000 kilometers or 13,620 miles in length when one considers every mile of deeply indented channels called fjords and all of the islands. This same action occurred along the coastline of Alaska and British Columbia as well as in southern Chile and on South Island New Zealand. And today fjords are being carved by glacial action on Greenland and Canada's Baffin Island. But of all the glacially created fjords, none have the combined physical and cultural magnificence of those in Norway. This is not to say that the other fjords are not beautiful because of course they are. But there is a quality to the Norwegian fjords that is hard to match, even harder to put into words.

Most of southern and central Norway is covered in dense forest, the same coniferous forest that stretches into Russia, known as the taiga. Stands of spruce, pine and willow dominate the lower elevations, as at these northern latitudes the tree line is not very high above sea level. However, in the far north, above the Arctic Circle where the long winter climate is harsh, the landscape is one of tundra, essentially a polar desert. Norway's population clings to the shoreline and occupies the small valleys in between the higher peaks, but this leaves them with very little land that is good for farming. Yet the Norwegians are excellent farmer, working what they have to produce dairy products, fruits and vegetables.

Norway is rich in raw material resources. It is obvious that timber has been one resource, but the North Sea shoreline is exceptionally well endowed with reserves of oil and natural gas. There are also deposits of copper, lead, zinc and titanium that have added to Norway's overall mineral wealth. However, to mine these resources, the Norwegians have been forced exploit remote mountain areas, and for the extraction of oil and natural gas they have had to build some of the tallest off shore drilling platforms ever constructed. Norway is also well known for its shipbuilding and fishing industries, thus the technology was there to turn to building oil-drilling platforms. Many ocean liners and cargo ships have been built in Norway, and Norwegian corporations have invested heavily in the shipping industry.

Norway is a country dominated over by winter. Around the Atlantic coastal margins rain rather than snow predominates because of the moderating influence of the warmer waters of the Gulf Stream. But even at sea level, the winter has periods of time that experience occasional heavy snow showers. The climate is said to be maritime, influenced heavily by the sea. The mountains and the interior experience cold winter temperatures and heavy snowfall. And most of Norway experiences little to no daylight for approximately two months in the middle of winter. Summer days are long; full 24 hours north of the Arctic Circle. And temperatures are mild, but along the coast there is still frequent rainfall, occasional fog and many days where there is no sunshine. Many coastal communities average only about 30 percent of the days in a calendar year during which there will be sunshine.

With a wet climate and high rugged mountain slopes, Norway is blessed with fast flowing rivers and streams, most flowing with tremendous force of white water rapids. Where rivers plunge over the glacially carved walls of the fjords, thousands of waterfalls add to the overall drama of the landscape.
At these northern latitudes during the long winter nights, Norwegians are treated to an

incredible light show, as the Aurora Borealis; also known as the Northern Lights, dance across the sky. Many visitors wait until the deepest part of winter and willingly brave the cold, rain and snow to have an opportunity to witness this phenomenon so widely associated with Norway. But of course it is also visible in neighboring Sweden as well as in Finland, Russia, Alaska, Canada and Greenland.

Tourism plays a significant role in the Norwegian economy. During the summer, there are increasingly more and more cruise ships that offer tours along and through the fjords. Also the extensive Norwegian ferry system transports tens of thousands of European and American visitors along this spectacular coastline, some coming by automobile and combining road and ferry to explore even the most remote of those fjords that are serviced.

The small and rugged mountains along the coast near Bergen

Small shelves of gentle land for farming on the offshore Lofoten Islands

A thundering white water river flows past the village of Hellesylt

The lower reaches of the Geiranger River just above e Geiranger Fjord.

The spectacular beauty of Næroyfjorden in central Norway

The upper reaches of the Valley of Fläm that was glacially carved

The high glacially sculpted mountains above Olden on Nordfjorden

The inside passage north of the city of Tromsø at midnight

The high and bleak tundra landscape of Magerøya Island on the Arctic shore

The Sámi people graze their reindeer on the Arctic islands and peninsula

A NORWEGIAN HISTORY

To best understand the culture and the landscape of any country you visit, it is important to know something of its history. It is the course of history that molds the culture and creates the visual landscape with regard to both the physical and human elements seen. Architecture, transportation networks, land use patterns and the amount of natural forest or grassland are all impacted by the succession of events that took place in the past. Humans are players on a stage, interacting with the props that are available and creating an ever changing stage set. And for this reason history plays a major role in what the visitor encounters. In the case of Norway, this is an old country with its history extending back beyond the 9th century, yet as a modern nation, it only dates to 1905.

To many prospective visitors, the name Norway is often synonymous with those northern warriors known as the Vikings. In essence it is their history that is the starting point for any written account of Norwegian timelines, yet there were earlier fishing and hunting tribes living along its shores dating back into prehistoric times long before our calendar. Despite the Hollywood image of the Vikings as warriors who terrorized and pillaged the shores of northern Europe, there were also merchants who engaged in legitimate trade, and colonists who set out from their cold, windswept lands to find more suitable homes.

Initially the Viking populace was scattered into tribal groups, each with its own chief of king. But in 872, much of the country was united under King Harald Hårfagre, this being the start of what would become a powerful force in Scandinavia. The Vikings adhered to their traditional "pagan" beliefs, but by the 11th century, Christian teaching had ultimately converted the majority, also helping to stem their raids on the nations along the North Sea.

The Kalmar Union, which was propagated by the Danes in 1350, ultimately united Norway and Sweden into one confederation, which was under the rule of the Danish king. But the Swedes rebelled in 1523 and left the Union because of their dissatisfaction with the power of the Danish crown. This break up was not without its share of bloodshed. Norway then became relegated to the status of a mere Danish province, something the Norwegians greatly resented. This displeasure festered until 1814, when Denmark, having lost a war with France, was forced to surrender Norway to Swedish rule. The Norwegians had drafted a constitution for their independence, but although forced into union with Sweden, many provisions of that draft were put into effect, as Sweden gave Norway a certain degree of internal home rule and its own separate crown, but the king was of Swedish nationality

As a means of developing their nationalism, the Norwegian people turned inward and concentrated their efforts upon fostering greater interest in their cultural identity through the arts, music and other manifestations of what it meant to be Norwegian. But ultimately this led to a political interest in the creation of an independent nation, which finally came to fruition on 7th July 1905 when the Norwegian Storting declared the country separated from Sweden and that the Swedish crown no longer would be recognized. The Swedish government was livid and there were even calls for armed forces to be sent into Norway. But in the end, both countries held separate referenda, and Norwegian independence was approved.

Since there was no Norwegian royal house, it was decided to invite young Prince Carl of Denmark, son of King Christian IX, to become the king of Norway. Taking the traditional Norwegian name of Haakon, the new royal house was established. And King Haakon VII reigned until 1957. To the present day, King Haarald V is the true head of the royal family, but also shows pride in his close familial relationship to the Danish Royal Family.

Life for the average Norwegian during the 19th and early 20th century was hard, as the country's economy was based upon limited farming, timber extraction and fishing. Essentially Norway was a backward country and large numbers of the poor emigrated primarily to Canada and the United States. It has been estimated that well over half a million Norwegians left for the New World, and states such as Minnesota, North and South Dakota and the Canadian provinces of Ontario and Manitoba show significant Norwegian communities. As in many European countries, manufacturing plants were developing in the major cities, and for those peasants who left the land for the city, life remained hard, often more difficult because urban residents were not able to at least supplement their incomes with homegrown foods.

Unlike many countries in Europe that industrialized, Norway did have one ready source of power, that being hydroelectric that provided clean and affordable energy for both industrial and domestic use. Apart from shipbuilding, manufacturing of paper products and a few fine quality metallic implements, Norway did not become one of Europe's industrial giants.

Although Norway was not drawn into the First World War, its economy did feel the same degree of contraction during the global depression of the 1930's. At the outbreak of World War II, Norway was invaded by Nazi forces from Germany because it offered two important resources. Its hydroelectric facilities, especially in the southern part of the country, were necessary for the production of heavy water, a vital component for the possible creation of nuclear weapons. And secondly was Norway's coastline that fronted on the major warm water trade route to the far north of European Russia. Nazi submarines and planes could harass allied shipping meant to aid the Russians in its fight on the Eastern Front once Germany invaded the Soviet Union.

The German invasion of Norway overwhelmed the small Norwegian military and the country fell under Nazi occupation, but a strong resistance movement developed and was instrumental in thwarting many of Germany's strategic operations. Sweden offered refuge to the Norwegian freedom fighters along with Allied pilots and paratroopers who aided in operations against Nazi installations.

Germany established a puppet government under the leadership of Vidkun Quisling, a man whose very name became associated with being a traitor to one's own country. But the vast majority of Norwegians silently opposed German occupation even though Nazi propaganda tried to equate being Norwegian with being a part of their so-called "master race." The Viking heritage of Norway figured prominently into Nazi myth.

Modern Norway presents a totally different picture than it did in prewar years. After two decades of reconstruction and repair of many damaged bridges, roads and harbor installations because of the war, Norway was soon back to a level of economic stability. The country took its place in the modern world as a member of the United Nations and later of the North Atlantic Treaty Organization.

The biggest single boost to Norway was the discovery of oil and natural gas in large underwater reserves off the coast, but within Norwegian territorial limits. As a result, the country with its small population began to see great sums of money coming into its treasury. Rather than utilizing the money for infrastructure or squandering it on monumental constructs, Norway invested the money in global programs for the benefit of its citizens in a national pension program. Today Norway's pension program is the envy of the world, and every one of its citizens has a secure future ahead. Infrastructure development, medical and educational services and other government programs are financed through high levels of taxation while the pension program is the beneficiary of the petroleum and gas profits. Even with the current low prices for fossil fuels, Norway is secure. However, jobs in the petroleum and gas industry have diminished, and this has caused unemployment that then strains the government's welfare programs.

Overall life in Norway is good. There is equal pay for men and women, excellent health and welfare benefits, and the country has a strong educational system available to all citizens. Yet Norwegians are not overly indulgent and the average family lives a comfortable lifestyle without being extravagant, as seen among other oil rich nations. Norwegians hold the natural environment to be very special, and they enjoy their country's beauty and recreational potential. It is true that there is no "Eden" on this earth, but Norway is one of those countries where life can be described as almost idyllic.

Akershus Castle in Oslo dates to 1290 AD

Hanseatic League buildings in Bergen date to the 14th century

On the back streets of Bryggen in Old Bergen

The old village church in Geiranger

The old village church in Olden

Interior of the old village church in Olden

OSLO - THE NATIONAL METROPOLIS AND CAPITAL

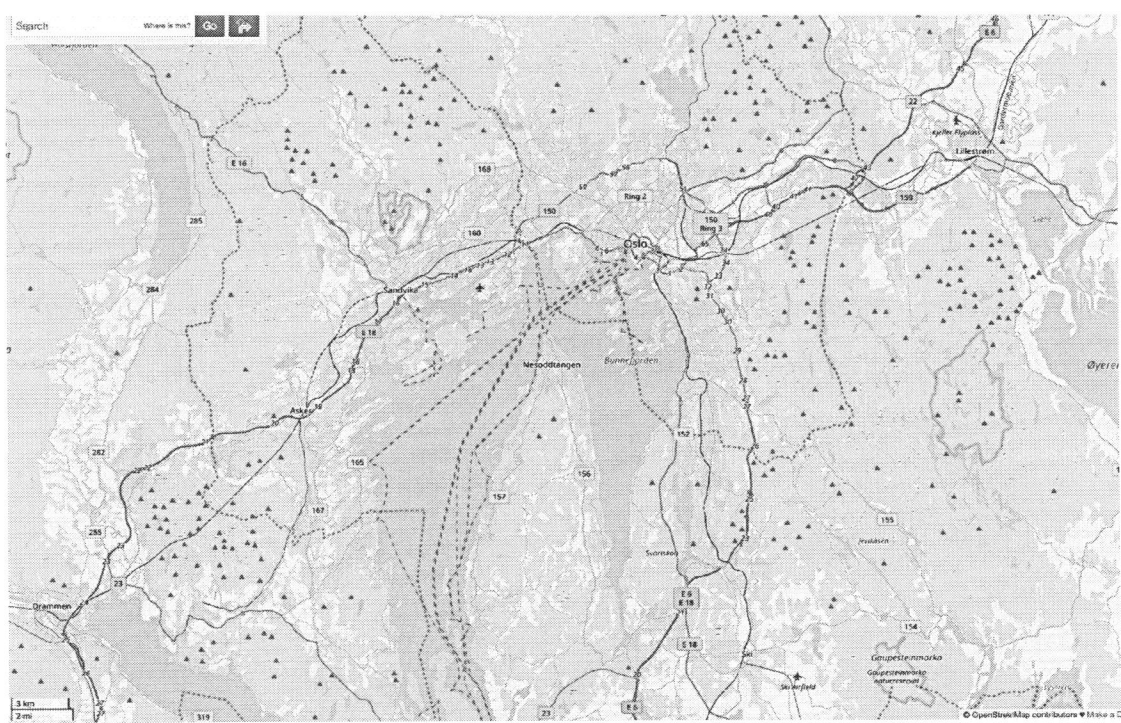

Oslo Fjord and the city of Oslo. (© OpenStreetMap contributors)

The majority of cruise ships do not visit Oslo as often as the other major cities of Scandinavia or the Baltic Sea region. Many cruise lines use Copenhagen as their port of embarkation for fjord cruises, as it is closer to the main travel route at sea. Oslo is actually not a convenient location to begin or end a fjord cruise because it is not on any major sea routes. The city's location is not as pivotal as Copenhagen or Stockholm in the planning of cruise itineraries. A visit to Oslo often involves one day or a half-day at sea at both the front and back end of the port call because of its location easily worked into a seven or 10-day cruise schedule.

THE SETTING FOR OSLO: Norway's capital is located approximately 130 kilometers or 80 miles up the long and narrow Oslofjord, which was created by glacial action during the Pleistocene or Ice Age. The journey up the fjord as well as back out after visiting the city is one of the highlights of visiting Oslo by ship. There are many small villages with their whitewashed wood houses that cling to the forested hillsides overlooking the fjord. It takes around three hours sailing time to reach the city or the Skagerrak on the return voyage. And if the weather is good, sitting out on deck and watching the passing countryside is richly rewarding, as it gives you a good glimpse into life in coastal life in the more populated portion of southern Norway.

Oslo occupies a crescent shaped bowl set amid thickly wooded hills at the upper end of Oslofjord. There are also numerous small islands within the fjord that belong to the city. Surrounding Oslo, the countryside is gently rolling and dotted with many fresh water lakes set amid mixed forests of broadleaf deciduous trees and conifers. Oslo is a picturesque, spotlessly clean yet modern city, reflecting both the past and forward look of the Norwegian people. Oslo has a population of only 560,000 and with its suburbs, it contain approximately 1,000,000 people, but the city gives the appearance of being a large town rather than a major city. The heart of Oslo hugs the shoreline at the top of the fjord, surrounded by spacious suburbs that extend into the surrounding hills and along both shorelines of the fjord. There are now a few high-rise buildings along the waterfront and in the newer east end of the city center. The city also possesses a myriad of parks and gardens, all combining to give Oslo the feeling of being far less urbanized than it truly is. Unlike Stockholm or Copenhagen, there are more single-family houses in Oslo than the other two larger capitals. The majority of the houses in Oslo, and for that matter in all of Norway, are constructed of wood siding, generally painted white. A front porch is commonplace and the houses are set in small, but impeccably landscaped lots that show how much Norwegians care about their homes. And it is this flavor rather than the proliferation of apartment blocks that lends the aura of being in a small city rather than a major capital. This illusion is especially noticeable after first visiting Copenhagen or Stockholm where the apartment block predominates.

Oslo summer weather is just about perfect with regard to temperatures that are in the 20's Celsius or upper 60's to mid 70's Fahrenheit. There are many rainy or cloudy and drizzly days, but around half the time the sky is blue and there is just a light breeze. However, winter weather can be cold, blustery with a mix of rain and snow. But there are no pleasure cruises at this time.

THE HISTORY OF OSLO: Oslo's heritage is that of the Vikings. Archaeological evidence shows that there were inhabitants in the area well before the end of the first millennium, yet Norse legend tells of the city having been founded in 1048 by King Harald Hardråe as a local trade center. So suffice it to say that Oslo is an old city. In 1261, King Håkon IV brought Norway to its golden age, forming a union with Iceland and Greenland. Oslo did not become the capital of the kingdom until the reign of King Håkon V (1299-1319). He is known to have been the first king to have actually taken up residence in the city, which was initially known as Christiana, later spelled Kristiana. The name was not changed to Oslo until 1925. To this day, the meaning of the name is unclear. It has been used as a boy's name but there is no single definition to its meaning. Several sources do say that it is taken from ancient Norse, and possibly means the meadow of the gods.

As Oslo grew in importance, its deep-water port closer to the interior heartland of the country with easier access first by road and later by rail slowly took away Bergen's significance as a port. And ultimately Bergen lost its role as the capital. Today Bergen is Norway's second city both in population and importance.

By the 14th century, Norway would be drawn into the Kalmar Union with Denmark. And in 1814, Norway became tributary to Sweden until 1905, thus the political significance of Oslo was far less important than that of Copenhagen or Stockholm. And this shows in the lack of many great stately buildings such as those found in the other two major Scandinavian capitals. The city was also primarily constructed of wood rather than stone or brick and it suffered numerous fires. The great 1624 fire actually caused the city to rebuild across the top end of the fjord where the city center is located today. The city rebuilt around Akershus Castle, which dates to the reign of King Haakon V who actually initially made Oslo the capital.

There is a less pretentious air about Oslo, as it still maintains its small city flavor. In 1814, when Norway once again became an independent kingdom in personal union with Sweden, the city began to take on more the feeling of an important center with the development of many public buildings, but to this day, it never lost its lack of pretention. The Royal Palace was built in 1848 and the Storting (national parliament) was built in 1866, the two most prominent buildings in the city center.

In 1952, Oslo played host to the winter Olympic games. These were the first post-World War II winter games to be held. Norway was host to the 1994 winter Olympic games, held just north of Oslo in Lillehammer. This brought the focus of a lot of media attention to Oslo, as well as hundreds of thousands of visitors since the capital is also the major transport hub of the nation. Oslo was the city that Olympic athletes and visitors had to fly into, and then travel by train to Lillehammer. Despite its mountainous terrain, Norway does possess a significant railway system, and of course Oslo is the railroad hub of the country.

During World War II, Oslo became the seat of power for the puppet government under Nazi control. Freedom fighters were more active in sabotaging Nazi military installations rather than attacking many sites within the capital. But Nazi forces held a tight grip on the city, and its Jewish population, which was the largest in the country, was deported to concentration camps and few ever returned.

Since World War II, Norway has been considered one of the most peaceful and safest countries in Europe. But in summer 2011, a young Norwegian terrorist set off a large bomb in the government section of the city and then he opened fire on a group of young people at a summer camp on one of the islands in Oslofjord, killing 68 and wounding over 100. This was a catastrophic blow to national identity, as something like this could never have been anticipated in Norway. Fortunately there have been no further such homegrown terrorist acts committed in the country.

HOTELS IN OSLO: If you are on a cruise that either embarks or terminates in Oslo, your cruise will not include any tours of the city. I strongly recommend that you plan to spend a minimum of one day, preferably two if possible, as this is a beautiful city worthy of your time. There are so many excellent sights to take in and its overall atmosphere represents the best of the urban lifestyle in Norway. To this end, I am recommending the following hotels as premier accommodation, offering the top level of comfort and elegance:

* Grand Hotel Oslo - Located in the heart of the city on Karl Johanes Gate #31, this is the most famous and venerated hotel in the city, similar to that of the Grand Hotel Stockholm. It is an expensive hotel, but you must keep in mind that it offers all the five-star amenities one would expect. The hotel offers outstanding dining, room service, spa, fitness center and concierge services. It has always been my choice when staying in Oslo. I rate it *****

* Hotel Continental - In the city center at Stortinsgata #24-26, this is a five-star property, but smaller than the Grand Hotel. It offers the same quality of dining with breakfast included in the room tariff. All the services one expects from a premier hotel are provided. The room rates are higher than most other hotels, but you must keep in mind this is based upon the quality of overall services offered.

* The Thief - This is another five-star hotel, but one that is quite modern in its overall decor. It is more of a boutique property with only 118 rooms and suites, located at Landgangen #1. The room tariff includes full breakfast. The hotel offers fine dining, a business center, indoor pool, concierge service and airport transportation. Its location in Aker Brygge is one of the most popular sections of the city for restaurants, bistros and clubs. This could be considered as the most "hip" part of Oslo for those into nightlife.

* Thon Hotel Rosenkrantz - Located in the city center at Rosenkrantz # 1, the hotel is right in the heart of all the major sightseeing and dining venues within a short walk of the front door. This is a four-star property with rates that are slightly lower than the five-star properties noted above. Breakfast is included in the room tariff. The hotel offers fine dining, a fitness center and gym, full business center.

SIGHTSEEING IN THE CITY OF OSLO: When cruise ships are in port, their shore arrangements include city tours of Oslo, visiting many of the highlights. But if you choose to see the city on your own, you will find that public transport is quite good. Within the central part of the city there are numerous tramlines, and conductors can easily direct you to where you want to go since English is widely spoken. There is also an extensive commuter rail network that you can utilize to visit those few important venues that are out beyond the central city, especially the major Olympic ski jump facility in the hills above the city.

Although Oslo is a comparatively small city as seen on the maps in this chapter, it is filled with wonderful museums, galleries and parks. Being compact makes getting around easier than in some of the larger cities of the Baltic Sea region. Most of the city's main attractions are close to the waterfront around which the central downtown is built. Many of the important landmarks of Oslo include:

* Aker Brygge – the city's main central square, which faces the quay and the busy harbor. The way Oslo's downtown area radiates out from the harbor; it shows the importance of the docks to the city's overall economic well-being. Today many modern apartment and condominium blocks have spread out along the waterfront from the main square. There are also many restaurants and bistros making this a very lively district at night. It has become very popular both with locals and visitors alike.

* Akershus – the great fortress palace that once defended Oslo. It dates to the days when warfare was a major fact of life. Most cruise ships dock along the waterfront right at the base of the fortress, making it an easy venue to visit either at the start or end of the day's activities. The castle is open daily from 6 AM to 9 PM, located right on the waterfront overlooking where cruise ships dock.

* Domkirke – the major cathedral of Oslo. Like all of Scandinavia, Norway is a strictly Protestant country, primary Lutheran. Visitors are welcome except on days when there are special events or services, but no hours are posted.

* Fram Polar Ship Museum - This museum contains a major ice breaking exploration vessel and exhibits honoring Norway's polar explorations. The address is Bygdøynesveien # 39. During the summer season the museum is open from 0 AM to 6 PM daily.

* Holmenkollen Ski Jump and Museum - Located in the hills above the city, accessed by train from the city's main station, this is a must see venue. The Olympic ski jump itself is dramatic to view from up close. On a clear day, the view from Holmenkollen is magnificent. Holmenkollen can be reached from Central Station by commuter train to Kongeveien. It is open between 10 AM and 4 PM daily.

* Karl Johan Gate - This grand boulevard runs from the heart of the city's shopping district past the Norwegian Parliament to Oslo University and the Royal Palace. The park along the west side of the street has a large outdoor cafe that is a popular spot for a cold drink or snack.

* Kon Tiki Museum - Dedicated to the famous anthropologist Thor Heyerdahl, this museum features vessels from his famous expedition in 1947. More on this important expedition is noted at the end of the list of attractions in Oslo. The address is Bygdøynesveien 36, reached by ferry every 20 minutes from the city hall pier. During summer the museum is open from 9:30 AM to 6 PM daily.

* Museum of Norwegian Resistance - For anyone with an interest in the role of the underground opposition to Nazi rule during World War II, this museum should be on your list. It is not well known, but it does document the role of the resistance fighters. The address is Bygning #21. It is open between 11 AM and 4 PM daily.

* National Museum and National Gallery - Here you will find a good assortment of exhibits on Norwegian culture and art. Among the works of art is the world famous, but controversial painting by Edvard Munch entitled "The Scream. The museum is located at Universitetgate # 13 and is open from 10 AM to 6 PM Monday thru Wednesday, extended to 7 PM and open from 11 AM to 5 PM on weekends. Thursday and Friday The gallery is at Bankplassen # 3 and open from 11 AM to 5 PM weekdays and Noon to 5 PM on weekends.

* Norwegian Folk Museum - Here you can learn about the folk culture and arts and crafts of the Norwegian people. Much of the museum is open air and gives you the feel of walking through a traditional village. The museum is located at Museumsveien # 10 in the district of Bygdøy and is open from 10 AM to 6 PM daily during summer. It can be reached by ferry from the waterfront opposite the Rådhusto the dock at Dronning.

* Peninsula of Bygdøy - site of the most fashionable residences of Oslo. If you are on your own, I suggest simply walking around and just soaking in the atmosphere. There are many fashionable restaurants and bistros and the district is home to several museum venues. You can reach the peninsula by ferry from the waterfront opposite the city hall.

* Rådhus – the brick city hall, which dominates the heart of Oslo. Red brick is a popular building material throughout Scandinavia, since quarried stone is difficult to obtain. The building is open daily from 9 AM to 4 PM and guided tours are offered for groups of 30 or more if pre booked. The building stands along the waterfront and is the most dominant structure on the downtown skyline.

* Royal Palace – home to the King of Norway. There is a changing of the guard at midday and the palace gardens are open to the public. During summer guided tours are offered to

the public. Tours in English are offered at Noon, 2 PM, 2:20 PM and 4 PM daily. The public entrance is off Slottsgården on the west side of the building. The palace sits at the upper end of Karl Johanes Gate.

* Stortorvet – the city's bustling market area, offering the visitor a glimpse into the rich diversity of seafood and produce. It is located at Stortorvet # 1 near the main cathedral and is open daily between 9 AM and 6 PM.

* Stovnertårnet – This is a new observation pathway of unique design to view the city if it is a clear day. And in autumn, the surrounding trees are ablaze in full color. The pathway is 260 meters long and winds its way to a magnificent crest overlooking the city. The lookout can be accessed via the subway on lines 4 and 5 to Stovner and then the start of the walk is a short distance.

* Vigeland Museum - Adjacent to the park, this museum contains many of Vigeland's drawings and some of his marble sculptures. The museum is open Tuesday thru Sunday from Noon to 4 PM and is located at Nobeisgate # 32.

* Vigeland Sculpture Park – one of the city's major attractions with outdoor sculpture set amid lush greenery. Also known as Frognerparken, this massive park features hundreds of dramatic statues created by the master sculptor Gustav Vigeland. His view of mankind and its place in the world is quite distinctive and has won acclaim from art critics everywhere. The human figures depicted tell Vigeland's story of mankind, and you will either find that you can relate to his message or that you find it to be rather morose. There is little middle ground when it comes to the Vigeland Sculpture Park and how people react to it. The park is open 24-hours daily and is free to the public. It is easily reached by subway traveling west to Majorstuen Station.

* Viking Ship Museum - This may be a small museum, but it does have several well-preserved examples of early Viking ships and other artifacts to help explain these energetic explorers. The museum is open between the hours of 10 AM and 4 PM daily and is located on the Bygdøy Peninsula at Huk Aveny # 35.

As you can see, Oslo is a city of museums. There is something for almost every taste, and I have not identified all of the museums. The most famous of the museums for those who were young when Thor Hyerdahl sailed in his flimsy raft from Peru to French Polynesia, proving a possible link between the two, a visit to the Kon Tiki Museum is an absolute must because it enables you to see Thor Heyerdahl's original raft, the Kon Tiki, that he sailed from Peru to French Polynesia in the mid 1900's. Heyerdahl was also the one who built a reed boat called the Ra'a, and he sailed it from the mouth of the Nile River to Central America, attempting to show a connection between ancient Egypt and the Maya. He is considered to have been Norway's premier anthropologist, and although his views have met with skepticism among many in his discipline, his adventurous spirit has never been doubted by any of his colleagues around the world. Even at present, there are those who dismiss him as simply an adventurer while others praise his work as a breakthrough in understanding how cultural traits may have been diffused between far distant locations.

MAXIMIZING YOUR TIME: After looking at the list of Oslo sights, you may ask how it is possible to see a large number of the venues described and also get a feel for the city of Oslo. Frankly it is impossible unless your particular cruise itinerary begins or terminates in Oslo. Only a handful of such itineraries exist each summer. Normally cruise ships stay for a maximum of a full day, but clearly it is insufficient time to see more than a handful of sights. Many cruise lines offer an overview tour of the city, but I personally find these tours to be very superficial. They attempt to provide a driving excursion through the city with few opportunities to stop at take photos or absorb what you are seeing. These tours will include from one to possibly three major venues where you will be herded through rather rapidly. If you are not the adventurous type or have physical disabilities, yes these tours are the best option for seeing Oslo or any of the cities on your itinerary. As a geographer, I favor personal exploration by one of the following means:

* Hiring a car and driver for the day, either through the cruise line or arranged by your travel agency or hotel concierge if you are staying in the city prior or after your cruise. This gives you the freedom and flexibility to see the city on your terms, visiting the types of venues that suit your taste. This is a rather expensive way to visit any city, especially those in Scandinavia, but it does maximize your time.

* Hiring a taxi from the dock area is a less expensive way to have a personalized tour. In most Baltic Sea countries, you will find drivers who speak sufficient English or other languages to facilitate this type of exploration. Be sure to negotiate the price in advance as well as the method of payment.

* Utilizing local transportation can be challenging for most, but it is the more affordable way to get around on your own. Most city transport systems offer all day visitor passes. With a good map, some pre planning and patience, you can get around and have a rewarding day. Oslo does offer a good mix of trams, busses and a commuter rail network that will get you to all of the venues on the list above. There will be a local representative either on board or dockside to advise, or if you are staying in a hotel, the concierge will provide you with the necessary information.

* There are hop on hop off busses available in Oslo. The routes will include the major venues of the city and operators provide maps and narratives to help maximize your independent explorations. These busses will be available where your ship docks, or if you are staying in the city, your hotel concierge can advise as to the nearest stop.

DINING IN OSLO: Norwegian cuisine is heavily oriented toward seafood. Atlantic salmon is one of the country's great delicacies. One distinct Norwegian treat is gravlax. It is salmon that has been rubbed with sugar and dill, giving it a very distinct flavor through the way it is cured. Also on the menu is herring, an essential staple in the Norwegian diet, as are the very crisp flat breads made from rye flour. Gravlox and herring are often eaten on these flat breads, topped with a piece of cheese. Fiskeboller is my favorite hot entree. It is made with chopped fish bound together with egg and breadcrumbs and then poached in fish broth. Fiskeboller can be served either hot or chilled.

One Norwegian food item that many of us from the rest of the world may find difficult to accept is whale meat. I have tasted it by accident as part of a traditional buffet. It was prepared similar to meatballs. But when I tasted it and discovered that it was whale, I could not bring myself to eat it on general principle in that I believe whales are too magnificent to be slaughtered for food. But I must admit from the one bite I inadvertently tasted, it was very tender and flavorful, so I can understand why it is a popular food item. Essentially the much of the food of Norway is very similar to that of Sweden, but with a bit more emphasis placed upon seafood and of course the addition of whale meat. And as is true throughout Scandinavia, rich pastries and ice creams are a definite part of the Norwegian dessert menu.

I am only going to recommend a few dining establishments that specialize in traditional Norwegian cuisine based upon my personal experiences. My friends and relatives all chide me about being a food "snob." That may be true, but I simply like dining at restaurants that offer the very best in quality and service. And in foreign countries I like to find excellent restaurants that offer the taste of that country. For Oslo I have these recommendations:

* Fjord Restaurant - In the city center at Kristian Augusts gate # 11, this is a very popular restaurant with a truly Scandinavian menu that is heavily oriented toward seafood. Their dishes are beautifully prepared and served in a warm, friendly atmosphere. They are open only for dinner between 5 and 11:30 Pm Tuesday thru Saturday. But most cruise ships depart in the evening, so dinner is possible for many of you. Reservations are advised for dinner and the ship or hotel concierge can handle it for you.

* Grand Hotel Oslo - truly a grand hotel in every way, this venerable establishment is the city's number one hotel and it offers several world-class restaurants. For those on a cruise that will not be staying through the evening, I recommend the Grand Cafe, which faces out onto Karl Johan Gate. You have your choice of menu service or a buffet of delicious and traditional open face sandwiches. And when it comes to dessert, they offer a fantastic dessert buffet that will delight any sweet tooth. The cafe serves lunch and dinner. For a more elegant atmosphere, try Palmen, the main dining room for lunch or dinner. The cuisine is Norwegian and based upon the freshest ingredients of the season. Lunch, afternoon tea and dinner are served. The Grand Hotel is located on Karl Johan Gate opposite Parliament. Reservations are advised for dinner.

* Hos Thea - one of the finest restaurants in Oslo, specializing in Scandinavian dishes as well as cuisine from other parts of northern Europe. Hos Thea is elegant and the service is impeccable. However, unless your ship is staying late you may not be able to dine here, as they are only open from 5 to 11 PM for dinner. Located at Gabelsgate 11 in central Oslo. Have your ship or hotel concierge reserve a table for you.

* Maaemo - Located at Schweigaards gate # 15B, in the city center, this is truly one of the finest dining establishments in Oslo. It is elegant and expensive, but five-star quality food and service make it worthwhile. The traditional Scandinavian menu features a variety of meats, poultry and seafood all beautifully presented. Hours for dinner are Tuesday thru Friday 6 PM to 1 AM, Saturday 11 AM to 3 PM for lunch and 6:30 PM to 1 AM for dinner. Have your ship or hotel concierge call for reservations.

* Statholdergaarden - A restaurant with 200 years of history located in an old house with nearly 400 years of antiquity, the atmosphere is superb, romantic for those who have that taste in mind. And the food is outstanding; once again they specialize in Scandinavian cuisine. Located in the central city at Radhusgata 11, and only open from 6 PM to Midnight

for dinner. Ask your ship or hotel concierge to reserve a table for you.

* VulkanFisk - Located at Vulkan #5 in the district of Mathallen, this is a superb seafood restaurant featuring a broad menu of traditional Norwegian dishes all beautifully prepared. You will need to take a taxi to reach the restaurant, as it is too far northeast of the city center to walk. It is open Tuesday thru Thursday from 10 AM to 9 PM, Friday and Saturday from 10 AM to 10 PM and Sunday from 11 AM to 7 PM. They are known for their fabulous fish soup. And yes, as in so many seafood restaurants they do serve whale. A reservation is advised and your ship or hotel concierge can handle it for you.

SHOPPING IN OSLO: Oslo is an expensive city in which both to dine and shop. Norway has one of the world's highest standards of living and oil revenues have added to the overall expense of living in or touring the country. There are several shopping venues in Oslo, but North Americans in particular will find the costs quite high. Apart from the normal tourist kitsch, there are fine quality woolens, hand knitted sweaters and very excellent quality Scandinavian made clothing, but you will pay top Kroner. When I first started to visit Scandinavia every summer, I did not pay much attention to shopping, as few men do. But one summer I noticed that in all the cities there were major July sales. That year I bought several pair of Swedish and Danish made jeans and sport shirts. I was so pleased with the quality and style that now each summer when I am in Scandinavia, I make shopping for clothes a major activity. For men the Scandinavian brands such as Sand, Tiger, J. Lindberg and Johansen are outstanding and well worth the expense. Sorry I do not have any experience with women's clothing, but I have noticed that Scandinavian women always appear to be stylish and well dressed. I do know that Sand and J. Lindberg also produce a line of very stylish women's casual clothing. The major shopping venues are:

* Eger Karl Johan - a smaller, but very fashionable store offering primarily clothing and accessories with an emphasis upon Scandinavian brands. It is located right on Karl Johan Gate 23. Hours are from 10 AM to 7 PM Monday thru Wednesday and Friday, and from 10 AM to 8 PM Thursday. Saturday hours are from 10 AM to 6 PM.

* Glas Magasinet - the largest and oldest department store in central Oslo, this beautiful store offers a broad variety of merchandise. It also offers a department featuring traditional Norwegian handicrafts. It is located at Stortorvet 9 in the city center. Hours are from 10 AM to 7 PM weekdays and from 10 AM to 6 PM Saturday.

* Karl Johan Gate - This is the main shopping street, especially south of the Parliament, is where many of the finest shops in Oslo will be found.

* Oslo City Shopping Center - located opposite the central railway station at Stenersgaten 1, this is a collection of fashionable, but pricey shops. Hours are from 10 AM to 9 PM weekdays and 10 AM to 8 PM Saturday.

* Steen and Strøm Magasin - this is Oslo's other major department store that offers many fashionable Scandinavian brands for both men and women. It is located on Nedre Slottsgate 8 in the city center. Hours are from 10 AM to 7 PM weekdays and 10 AM to 6 PM Saturday.

FINAL WORDS: Although Oslo is one of the smaller capitals of Scandinavia, it is a city that is rich in history, strong on pride and especially beautiful in a rather laid back manner. There are no grand boulevards or imposing monumental buildings, as is true in Stockholm. What Oslo lacks in grandeur it makes up for in charm.

OSLO CITY MAPS

MAP OF CENTRAL OSLO

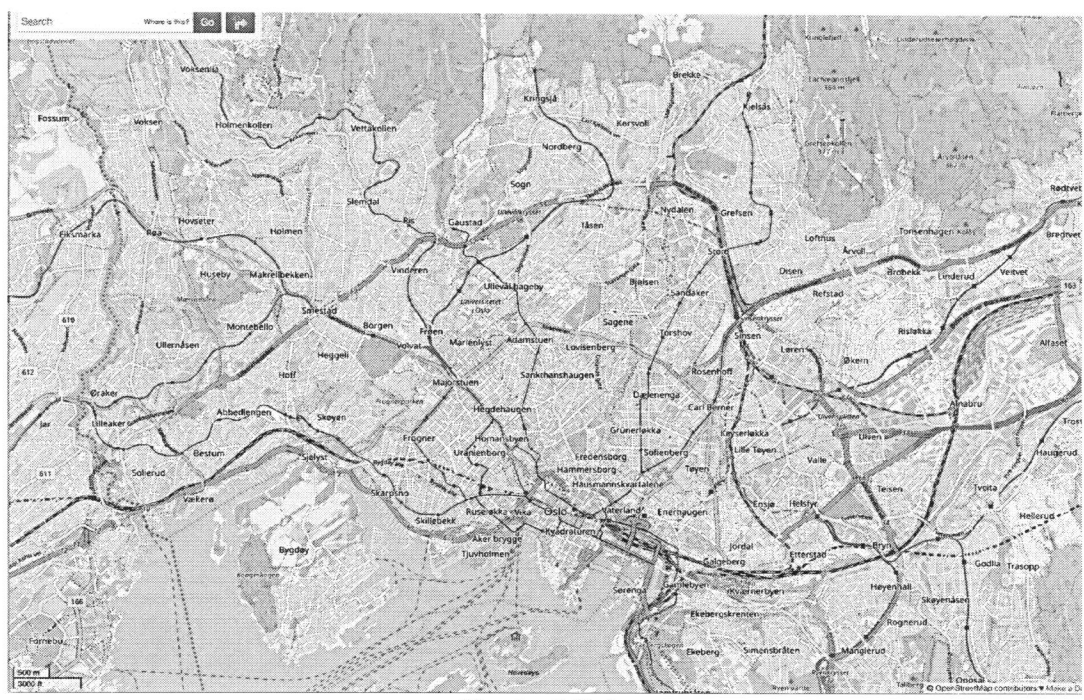

Central Oslo

This map is best viewed directly from OpenStreetMap.com on your personal device where it can be expanded or one specific area can be enlarged. Given the format of this book, it is impossible to display maps with the level of detail you might wish to have while actually out exploring the city. But the OpenStreetMap maps used directly are the tool I always rely upon.

MAP OF THE HEART OF OSLO

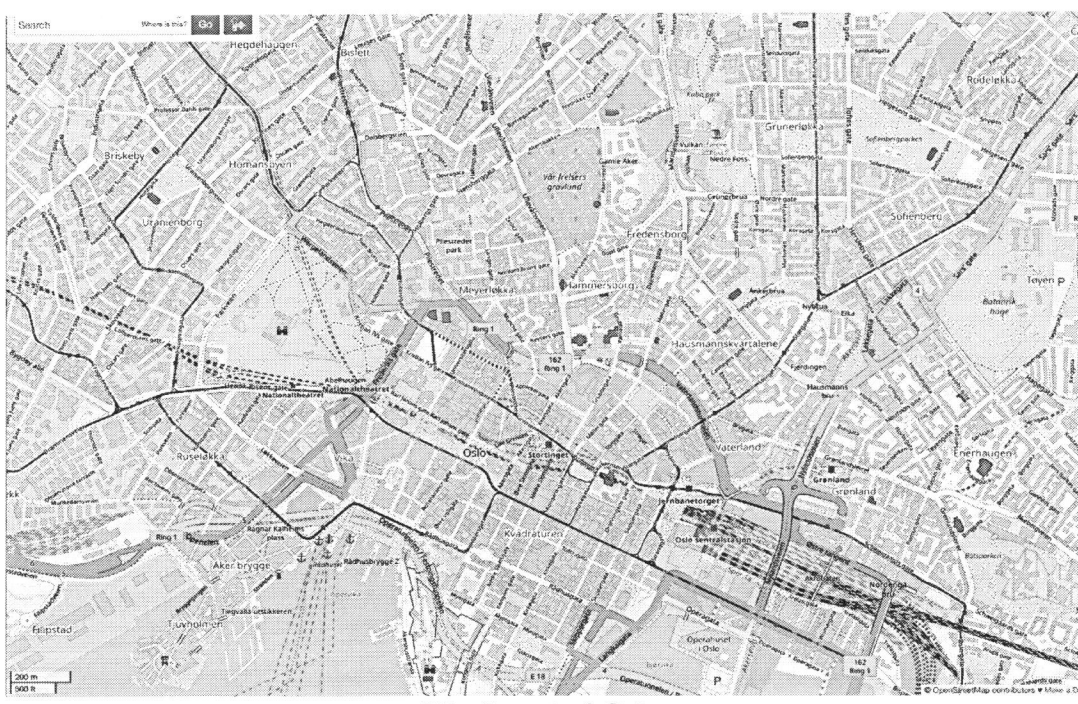

The heart of Oslo

This map is best viewed directly from OpenStreetMap.com on your personal device where it can be expanded or one specific area can be enlarged. Given the format of this book, it is impossible to display maps with the level of detail you might wish to have while actually out exploring the city. But the OpenStreetMap maps used directly are the tool I always rely upon.

MAP OF AKER BRYGGE DISTRICT

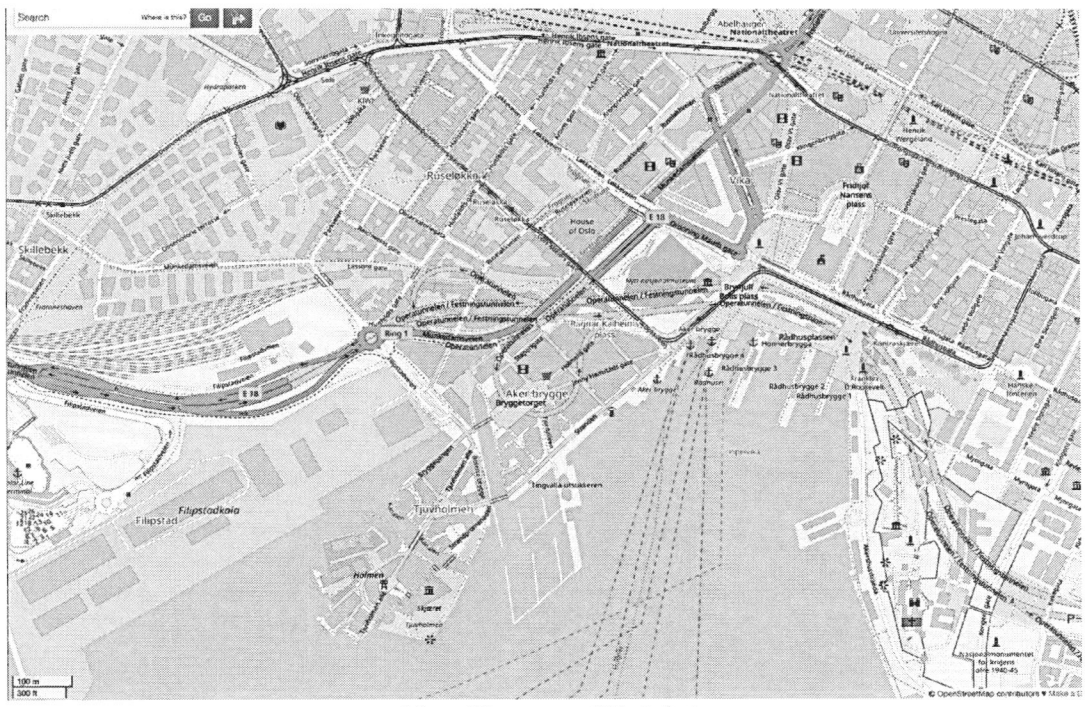

Aker Bryggen District

This map is best viewed directly from OpenStreetMap.com on your personal device where it can be expanded or one specific area can be enlarged. Given the format of this book, it is impossible to display maps with the level of detail you might wish to have while actually out exploring the city. But the OpenStreetMap maps used directly are the tool I always rely upon.

MAP OF VIGELAND SCULPTURE GARDEN AREA

Vigeland Sculpture Garden area

This map is best viewed directly from OpenStreetMap.com on your personal device where it can be expanded or one specific area can be enlarged. Given the format of this book, it is impossible to display maps with the level of detail you might wish to have while actually out exploring the city. But the OpenStreetMap maps used directly are the tool I always rely upon.

HOLMENKOLLEN SKI AREA

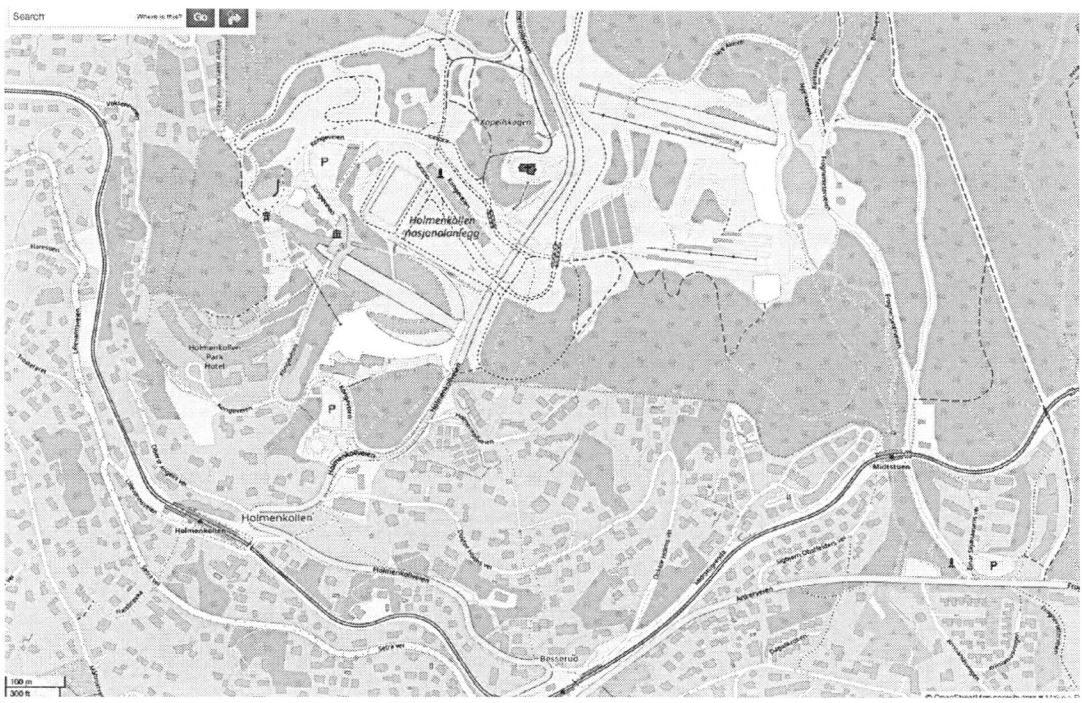

Holmenkollen ski area

This map is best viewed directly from OpenStreetMap.com on your personal device where it can be expanded or one specific area can be enlarged. Given the format of this book, it is impossible to display maps with the level of detail you might wish to have while actually out exploring the city. But the OpenStreetMap maps used directly are the tool I always rely upon.

One of the many picturesque villages along Oslofjord leading to Oslo

Approaching the city of Oslo by ship

A view of the Oslo skyline as the ship docks

The skyline of Oslo seen from Holmenkollen Ski Jump

Along the Oslo waterfront

Karl Johan Gate looking to the Royal Palace

The Grand Hotel on Karl Johan Gate

The old and new blend together in central Oslo

The Royal Palace of Norway

Henrikke Park along Karl Johan Gate

Fountains in Henrikke Park

The Norwegian Parliament

Saturday street life in central Oslo

Frogner Park and the Vigeland Sculpture Gardens (Work of Nick from Bristol, CC BY SA 2.0, Wikimedia.org)

Frogner Park covers expansive ground

An example of a typical small Norwegian wood house in Oslo

An example of elegant upscale housing near the Royal Palace

Poached salmon, boiled potatoes and cucumber salad at the Grand Hotel

STAVANGER

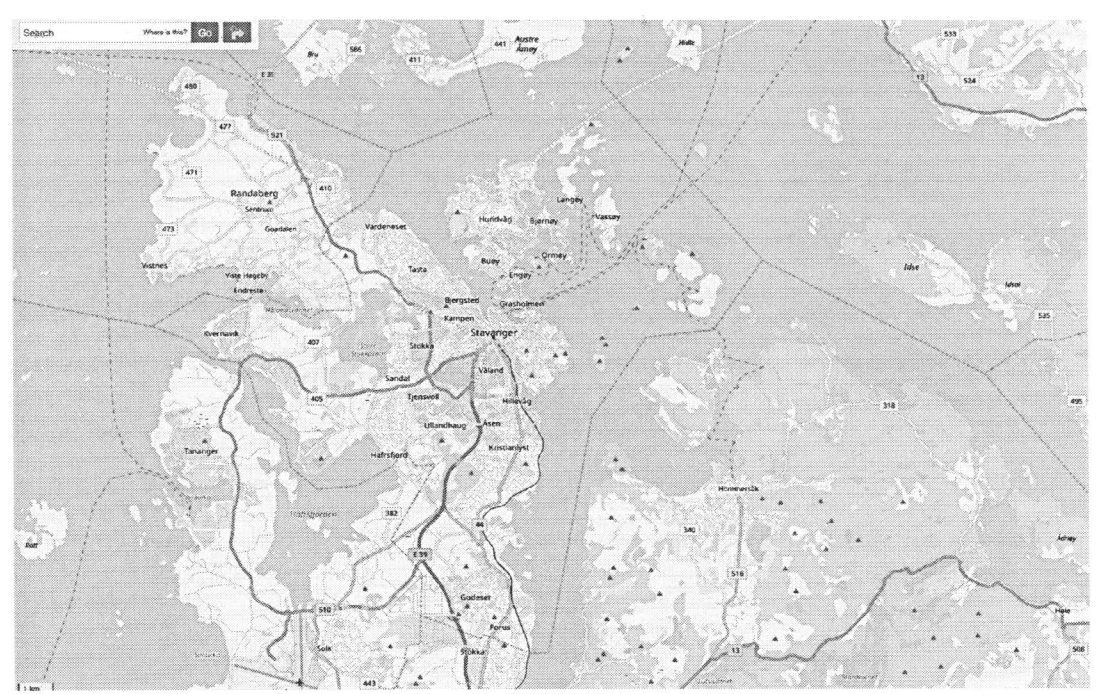

The greater Stavanger region. (© OpenStreetMap contributors)

THE CITY'S GEOGRAPHIC SITE: Stavanger is the fourth largest city in Norway with a current metropolitan population of approximately 300,000. Until recently, it was the third largest city in the country, but it has been slightly overtaken by the city of Trondheim, and their local residents are very proud of their new ranking much to the dismay of Stavanger residents.

The city is located on the west coast of Norway, facing to the storm prone North Sea in the southern part of the country. Stavanger sits on the more sheltered leeward side of a large peninsula that faces out into the North Sea. On the eastern side is the wide bay called Boknafjorden. This is essentially an outlet bay that was initially deepened by the coalescing of several smaller glaciers as they reached what was thousands of years back a lower sea level. The land is relatively low and gently rolling, the result more of glacial deposits rather than scour. And the region is also quite beautifully forested, the wooded areas interspersed with farmland that has been meticulously tended over the centuries. The magnificent fjord country that visitors expect to find in every port of call in Norway is found adjacent to Stavanger, but not in the immediate vicinity of the city.

The peninsula on which the city is built does have a somewhat hilly and rocky character, often typical of the mixed debris having been deposited during the periods of glaciation. There are also numerous offshore islands that represent portions of the mainland cut off by the coming together of many glaciers before reaching the sea.

The climate is typical of the maritime coast of all southern Norway. There are few winter days with temperatures below freezing, but rather hovering in the low ranges combined with much rainfall to create a chilly, rainy environment. Summers are very mild and daytime high temperatures are in the 20's Celsius or upper 60's to mid 70's Fahrenheit, and rainfall is also prevalent throughout the so-called warmer season. Yet surprisingly this is a productive region agriculturally because of the longer daylight hours combined with mild temperatures and plenty of precipitation. The southern coastal region is not known for many days when you will find blue skies and brilliant sunshine. But on those rare days, the landscape definitely has an added sparkle to it.

Few cruise itineraries visit Stavanger, and if you happen to be on a cruise that will be including this major city, do not hold great expectations for a blue-sky day, as they are relatively rare. This same condition will also hold true in Bergen. The southwest coast of Norway is one of the wettest parts of the country with there being more rainy days than sunny throughout the year. But it is all this rain that gives the region its lush, green landscape.

SETTLEMENT OF STAVANGER: The area around Stavanger has a long history of settlement even predating the history of the Vikings. There is actual evidence of the town dating back to the 11th century, having become an important market center and seat of church activity once Christianity was established in southern Norway.

The official date of founding is the year 1125 when the beautiful Stavanger Cathedral was completed and the first bishop came to serve the area. But the community existed well before its official founding It remained an important center of religious administration until the Protestant Reformation. In the early years of the 17th century, the bishop relocated to Kristiansand, and Stavanger then came to rely upon its local market role combined with the addition of the herring fishing fleet by the 19th century.

During World War II, the airport at Stavanger was bombed early in the morning of April 9, 1940, destroying the small Norwegian air contingent based there to protect this coastal region of the country. Within hours the Germans landed troops and supplies, the start of making this an important base of operation because of its strategic position facing out to the major sea traffic lane north to Murmansk in the Soviet Union. One of the most distinctive aspects of the German occupation of Stavanger was that in 1945 after the surrender, German soldiers were required by Norway to remain and remove all of the thousands of landmines that had been laid during the war.

When the Norwegians began to exploit their offshore oil reserves in the 1960's, it was recognized that Stavanger had two advantages, namely its large and deep harbor and secondly its proximity to the developing oil reserves, which were west and southwest of the city. As oil exploration expanded, other centers such as Haugesund, Bergen and Kristiansund also became important service centers for the oil drilling platforms. But Stavanger was the first, and it is still vital to the petroleum production industry. However, the decline in oil prices and the essential overproduction has caused a major degree of disruption to the industry. This has also caused the population growth rate and the overall economic output of the city to stagnate. And this is of course to the delight of the people of

Trondheim, allowing that city to gain the edge in that ongoing race to determine which is the country's third largest city.

THE CITY TODAY: Until recently, Stavanger was able to boast that it was the third largest city in Norway after Oslo and Bergen. It presently has a metropolitan area population of 319,000, but its city population is approximately 127,000. Trondheim is shown to have a city population of 176,000. But metropolitan Trondheim is still slightly below that of Stavanger according to most Norwegian sources. So in that ongoing race, the people of Stavanger still claim they are the third largest based upon metropolitan population.

As a visitor off of a cruise ship, there are many interesting sights in Stavanger, and of course most cruise lines have a variety of tours planned. I personally prefer to get out on my own, but that is because I have been to Norway around 20 times in the last ten years. If this is your first cruise through the fjords, then of course a tour in a small city like Stavanger will enable you to see all the major sights either in the city or the surrounding countryside, depending upon your preference.

As one of the oldest cities in Norway, there is a good degree of historic architecture, especially in the old town area. Although this was a well settled region during Viking times, as with all major Norwegian cities and towns, the emphasis architecturally is upon those elements of northern European tradition that were infused into the country with the coming of early Christian priests and merchant traders.

Stavanger sprawls along the water and into the hills behind the old city center. There is urban development on several of the small adjacent islands, connected to the central city by a network of small ferryboats. Most of Stavanger's residential districts are built of wood, a common building material in much of Norway because of the abundance of forests and the development of a forest industry. And the majority of the city's thousands of houses are painted white. Brick and stone tend to be reserved for public and commercial buildings rather than for individual homes.

Today there are many modern moderately tall apartment blocks lining the waterfront and the city center does possess a few contemporary skyscrapers, but nothing that would be exceptionally tall. Remember that this is a small urban center by overall European standards.

WHAT TO SEE AND DO IN STAVANGER: Here is my listing of the major sites worth your time while sightseeing within the city. And this is followed by the major locales outside of the city that can be visited within less than the usual six to eight hours that most cruise ships allow for Stavanger.

* Museum of Archaeology is located southwest of the city center, actually not too far south of the Cathedral. It is at Pedre Klowsgate #30-A and is also open only from 11 AM to 3 PM. Here you will find a good collection of artifacts and exhibits that portray the end of the glacial era along with the earliest evidence of human occupancy prior to the Viking culture. The museum also has a small cafe for quick meals.

* Norwegian Canning Museum - This museum presents the history of fishing for commercial canning and its role in the development of Stavanger. It is located along the narrow old harbor just north of the Old Town area at Oevre Strabdgate #88. It has limited hours between 10 AM and 4 PM daily.

* Norwegian Petroleum Museum - I recommend this only for those who are truly interested in the industrial history of the city and the important role played by North Sea oil. Located on the waterfront in the main dock area at Kjeringholmen # 1-a, it provides an insight into the oil and natural gas industry and what it means to Stavanger. Surprisingly, most visitors who are skeptical about visiting such a specific museum actually come away quite pleased that they visited. The museum is open daily from 10 AM to 4 PM with closing extended to 6 PM on Sunday.

* Old Town Stavanger - The old sector of the city with its tightly packed whitewashed wood houses lining narrow streets so typifies the older cities found along the Atlantic coast of the country. There are also many small shops and restaurants that have opened in the old sector because this has become a focus of cruise tourism because of its proximity to the waterfront. Many of the streets are now reserved only for pedestrians, but some are rather steep since much of the Old Town climbs the adjacent hills, which typify so much of the urban landscape. There are many words to describe the old sector such as quaint, picturesque, romantic or even fairytale like. It does give you a good picture of what urban Norway was like even at the start of the 20th century.

* Skagenkaien - Here along the waterfront you will find much of the early maritime architecture of the city, dating back to the founding of the port. And like the Old Town area, you will find Skagenkaien heavily oriented toward serving the tourists, especially on days when ships are in port. This area is also very close to where cruise ships dock, so for those with limited mobility, this is the easiest venue to visit.

* Stavanger Cathedral - Located at the edge of a beautiful parkland just to the southwest of the city center, this cathedral began as a Catholic center for the regional bishop. After an 18th century fire, the restoration of the main facade changed the entire look of the building, as under Protestant domination it was given more simplified lines. Originally this cathedral was closely tied to southern England, as it was English priests that first came to Stavanger in the 16th century. The cathedral is open during daylight hours for visitors unless there is a major event taking place.

* Stavanger Maritime Museum - Here you get a complete history with exhibits that relate Stavanger to the sea, and it is sure to please anyone who is interested in the role of sea commerce and the coast of Norway. It is located at the southern end of the old harbor at Strandkaien # 22 and also maintains limited hours from 11 AM to 4 PM daily. The museum does feature a good collection of replicas of small sailing vessels and early ships

* Swords in the Rock is an important monument to Norway's early history. It is located at Hafrsfjord on the southwestern edge of the city. The Norwegian name is Sverd i fjell. Without this being part of a tour, you will need to either have a private car or commission a local taxi on an hourly rate to get here. Or if you would like to try local transportation, city bus number 29 will bring you here from the city center. The monument consists of three hilts of old Viking

swords that protrude from solid rock in the same fashion as the famous Excalibur in the King Arthur legends. The monument celebrates a great battle fought in 872 in which Harald Harfagre was victorious and united most of the Viking tribes of Norway into a single nation. As an outdoor monument, it is open 24 hours a day all week and during summer with darkness coming around Midnight there is plenty of time to enjoy this monument.

* Valbergtårnet - This is the old watchtower standing on a high hill just to the east of the city center. In the days before any form of telecommunication, this was how the city protected itself by having watchmen on shift to look for the start of fires or even for the threat of outside invasion. Today it offers an outstanding close in view of the city center, giving the visitor some excellent photographic opportunities. Unfortunately at the time of this writing, no opening hours are posted online.

EXPLORING OUTSIDE STAVANGER: For those who want to explore some of the natural beauty of the countryside outside of Stavanger, there are two prominent locations that you can get to either as part of a ship sponsored tour or on your own with a private car or taxi. My recommendations are:

* Lysefjorden - If your cruise line offers a boat trip into Lysefjorden and if you want to truly see some magnificent scenery, then this is an option I would highly recommend. This narrow fjord located across the broad bay known, as Boknafjorden is a short distance from the city, yet it is a world away, as the fjord is narrow and the walls are steep, offering some beautiful photo opportunities.

* Vaulen Beach - Located just south of the city on the east side of the peninsula, Vaulen Beach is not quite the rugged out of door environment since it is still within the greater urban zone. But it does offer beautiful scenery of a rather placid nature, having calm waters, small groves of trees and surrounded by low hills albeit there are still some houses in view. But it is a nice retreat from the heart of Stavanger and is easily accessed by private car or taxi.

DINING OUT: Depending upon your cruise company's itinerary you may or may not have time for lunch. Many people prefer to skip an actual restaurant lunch and simply have a quick snack so as to not loose time. But I personally think that the dining experience is part of the adventure. So if you want to enjoy a traditional Norwegian lunch, here are my choices:

* 26 Restaurant and Social Club - In the city center at Loekkeveien # 26, this is a very popular restaurant that is noted for its fresh seafood served in a variety of traditional ways. The menu also offers many dishes for those who want to sample Norwegian cuisine, but who are not especially fond of seafood. For example they do present great burgers with a Norwegian twist. They are open for dinner Monday thru Thursday 6 to 10 PM, Friday and Saturday from 5 to 10:30 PM.

* Det Lille Hjornet - Located in the city center at Overe Holmegate #29 and open from 11 AM to 11 PM Monday, closing at Midnight Tuesday thru Thursday. On Friday and Saturday they are open from 11 AM to 2 AM and on Sunday from Noon to Midnight. This is my recommendation for those of you who just want a quick soup or sandwich or simply a dessert and tea or coffee. This is informal and service is quick so you can be on your way again to see more of the city.

* Dognville Burger - Located at Skagen # 13 in Old Town, this is a typical American grille that is noted for its hamburgers, something you do not find as commonplace in Norway. They also do feature vegetarian dishes as well. For those American passengers here is a chance to have a taste of home, especially if you are not partial to seafood, which so dominates. Hours of service are from 11 AM to 11 PM Tuesday thru Thursday, 11 AM to Midnight Friday and Saturday and Noon to 11 PM on Sunday.

* Fisketorget - Located in the city center at Strandkaien # 37 and open for lunch and dinner from 11 AM to 11 PM Monday thru Saturday, it is my first choice for traditional Norwegian seafood dishes. Two of the most popular dishes are a hearty fish soup and then followed by cod that has been sautéed with bacon. If cod is not to your taste, there are also choices ranging from salmon to whatever is the freshest catch of the day.

* Restaurant SOL - In the city center at Hetlandsgata # 6, this centrally located restaurant is noted as one of the best in Stavanger. Its menu features seafood, poultry and meats all prepared in a traditional manner and served in a charming atmosphere. It is so popular that it is best to have the ship concierge make a reservation. Their hours are Wednesday thru Friday from 5:30 to 10 PM, Friday 1 to 10 PM, Saturday 1 to 10:45 PM and on Sunday from 1 to 10 PM.

* Sjohuset Skagen - This very traditional restaurant is located in the city center as well, its exact address being Skagenkaien #13. It is open from 11:30 AM onward and specializes in seafood, which is of course what one expects in Norway. Their fish soup is said by many to be the best in Stavanger, but of course you must be the judge. They also serve whale meat, a very traditional dish in Norway. I have tried it, and yes it has a wonderful taste, but somehow I could not bring myself to go beyond just a taste, knowing it was whale. But again that is a decision you must make. They are open from 11:30 AM to 10 PM Monday thru Saturday and from 1 to 9 PM on Sunday.

* Tango Restaurant - At Nedre Strandgate # 25, this is an excellent traditional Norwegian restaurant that again is heavily into fresh seafood. The dishes are beautifully prepared and served in a friendly, but casual atmosphere. They are open Tuesday thru Friday 6 PM to Midnight and Saturday Noon to Midnight.

SHOPPING: Stavanger is not really a major shopping destination for cruise passengers, as it has primarily souvenir stores in the Old City. The most common item that people wish to buy is a hand knitted Norwegian sweater, and yes you will find a fair selection in the Old City area. But for a larger selection, I would recommend waiting until you get to Bergen unless you see something that you feel you absolutely must have.

FINAL WORDS: Stavanger is a beautiful city that typifies the gracious, yet not ostentatious lifestyle of the people of Norway. And as the country's third major urban region, it does offer all of the important services for its people and those in the hinterland. From a tourist perspective, there is a lot of historic architecture that will hold your interest.

CENTRAL STAVANGER

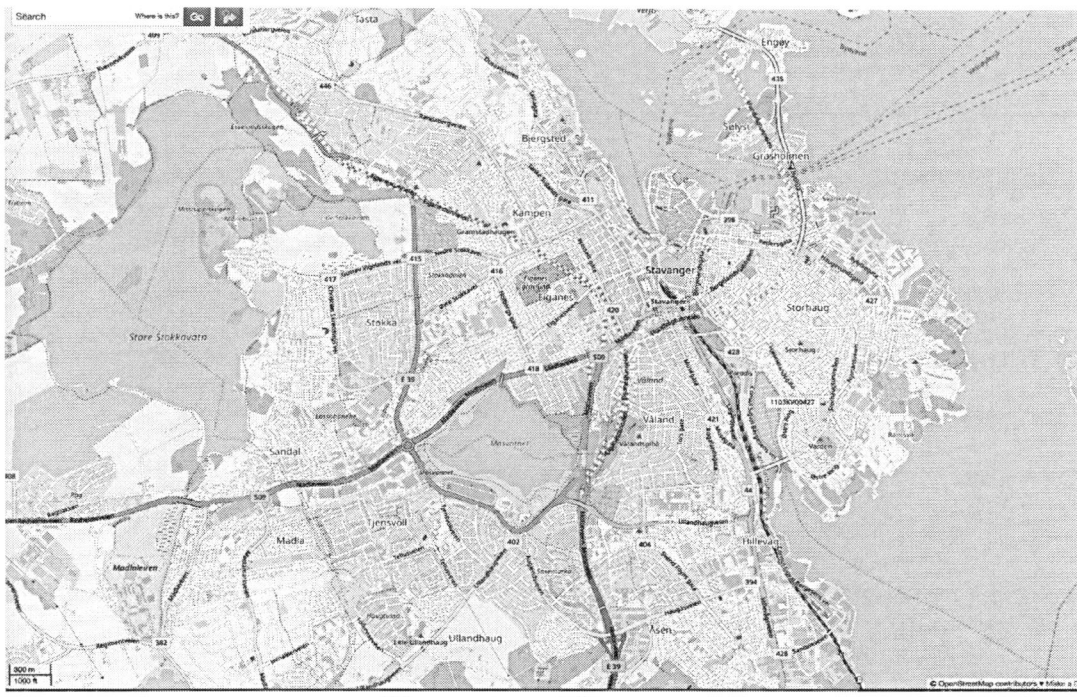

The center of Stavanger

This map is best viewed directly from OpenStreetMap.com on your personal device where it can be expanded or one specific area can be enlarged. Given the format of this book, it is impossible to display maps with the level of detail you might wish to have while actually out exploring the city. But the OpenStreetMap maps used directly are the tool I always rely upon.

THE HEART OF STAVANGER

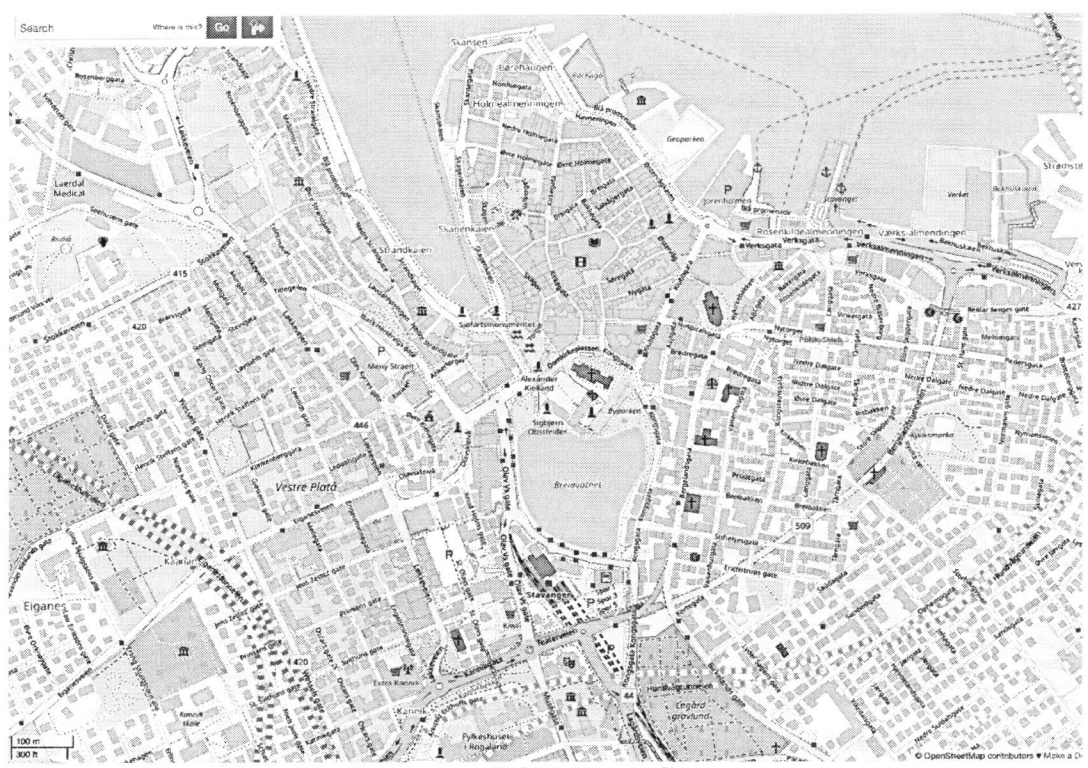

Downtown and Old Town Stavanger

This map is best viewed directly from OpenStreetMap.com on your personal device where it can be expanded or one specific area can be enlarged. Given the format of this book, it is impossible to display maps with the level of detail you might wish to have while actually out exploring the city. But the OpenStreetMap maps used directly are the tool I always rely upon.

A high altitude aerial over Stavanger looking to the southwest

An aerial over central Stavanger. (Work of Oyvind Rask, CC BY SA 4.0 Wikimedia.org)

Typical wood houses of Stavanger. (Work of Holger Uwe Schmitt, CC BY SA 4.0, Wikimedia.org)

The Stavanger waterfront. (Work of Holger Uwe Schmitt, CC BY SA 4.0, Wikimedia.org)

Central Stavanger, (Work of Michael Spiller, CC BY SA 2.0, Wikimedia.org)

In Old Stavanger, (Work of Trolvag, CC BY SA 3.0, Wikimedia.org)

In the heart of the older commercial center of Stavanger. (Work of Christian Bickel, CC BY SA 2.0, Wikimedia.org)

The modern side of Stavanger's waterfront. (Work of Zairon, CC BY SA 3.0, Wikimedia.org)

The old waterfront market area. (Work of Ranveig, CC BY SA 1.0, Wikimedia.org)

One of Stavanger's beautiful public gardens. (Work of Kilabas, CC BY SA 4.0 International, Wikimedia.org)

HAUGESUND

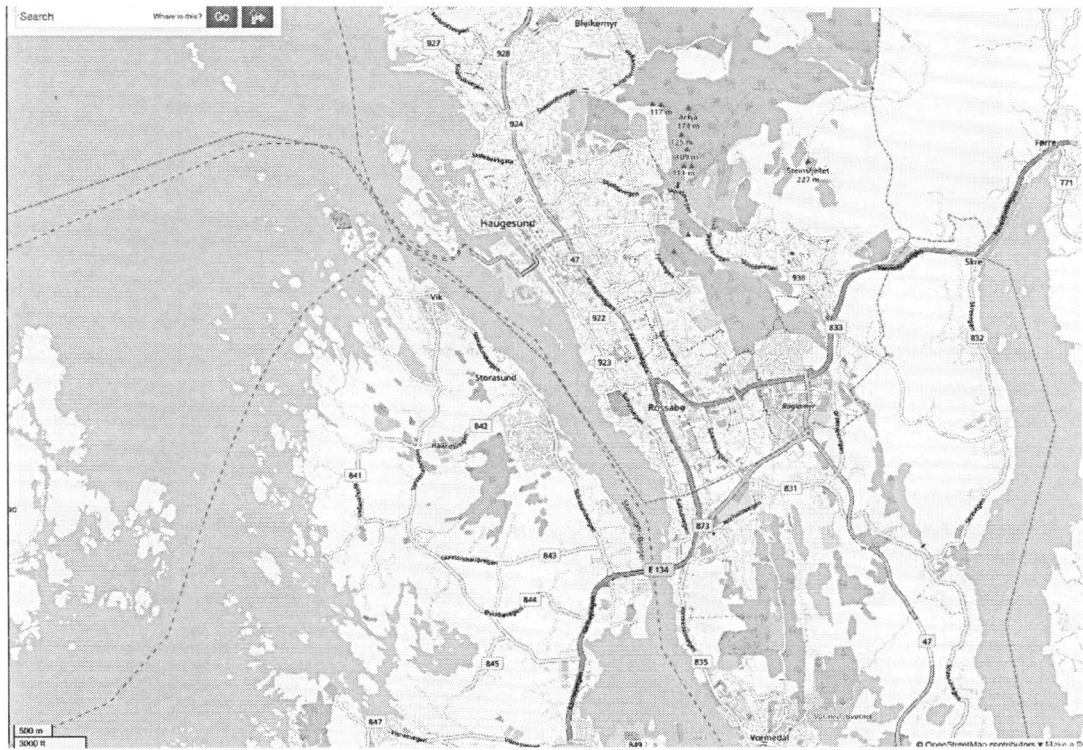

The Haugesund region (© OpenStreetMap contributors)

LOCATION: Haugesund is located just north of Stavanger but not many cruise ships seem to pay a port call, which I think is a shame because it is a delightful small city with a picturesque setting, wonderful architecture and delightful people. If your itinerary is fortunate enough to include Haugesund, you will find it an enjoyable visit. Both Haugesund and Stavanger seem to be missing from the majority of cruise itineraries. Time is normally the constraint with many Norwegian itineraries because of the distances involved and the emphasis being placed upon visiting the fjords rather than urban ports of call apart from Bergen.

The city is actually in a very strategic location because it lies at the northern end of the Karmsundet, a rather narrow, but deep inside passage that begins across the opening of Boknafjorden. Once passing through this channel and passing Haugesund, ships need only be in the open sea for another short stretch before they can enter another inside passage all the way to Bergen. Given the severity of the winter weather on the North Sea and also the occasional summer storms that can bring rough seas, the inside passages along most of the Norwegian coast has been a safe haven for ships plying the waters north and south between such ports as Arkhangelsk and Murmansk on the Barents Sea in far northern Russia and the Baltic Sea, which is reached after rounding the southern tip of Norway and passing between Denmark and Sweden.

The region surrounding Haugesund both on the large islands and the mainland is gently rolling to moderately hilly. The land where not cleared for agriculture consists of thick coniferous forests and the countryside is dotted with hundreds of glacial lakes while the coastline is indented with several fjords, both signs of intense glaciation. But although beautiful, it lacks the drama and majesty created by the higher mountains being closer to the sea, as found north from Bergen.

Climatically this area is within the maritime regime that dominates most of Norway until one gets beyond the Arctic Circle where a sub polar climatic regime begins. Winters are cold, hovering just around or above freezing and more rain than snow is commonplace. Thus blustery, damp and gray weather is the norm. Summers are very mild with daytime temperatures generally in the low 20's Celsius or upper 60's to mid 70's Fahrenheit., and with the warm offshore Gulf Stream, fog is quite common as the moist air loses its ability to hold the vapor, condensing it out into microscopic droplets suspended above ground level. The last time I visited Haugesund in 2016, it was a mild, almost warm, August day with blue skies, but by midafternoon a bank of fog came in from the open sea and visibility was reduced to almost zero in a matter of minutes. It was possible to just stand along the waterfront and watch the fog advancing like some alien miasma engulfing everything. It was quite hypnotic.

Haugesund is an important regional center for the surrounding farmland, fishing, servicing oil drilling platforms and fjord tourism. It is a very pleasant city with a population of 40,150 in its metropolitan area. The city presents both the feel of a small town, yet it has all of the important amenities of a city, including a well-developed business district, a beautiful cathedral, public buildings and parks. Like so many Norwegian cities, it is built on a series of hills, rising back from the waterfront and consists primarily of wood houses, most of them painted white. Public buildings are constructed of brick or stone, and many date to the late 18th and 19th centuries.

BRIEF HAUGESUND HISTORY: Like so much of southern Norway, archaeological evidence shows that there have been settlements in the region for many thousands of years, dating back to around 6,000 years ago. By the time of the Viking Era, starting in the 10th century, this was an important area for trade, including contacts across the North Sea to the British Isles.

The region is known as Rogaland, and it was an important Viking stronghold. A great battle for control of Rogaland took place in 872 when King Harald Fairhair was victorious and incorporated the area into his expanding Norwegian kingdom. The actual details of this victory are told in the Norwegian Sagas and some say they are as much myth as reality, somewhat like the stories of King Arthur and Camelot. A great monument, known as Haraldshaugen, was built in 1872 to commemorate the 1,000 anniversary of the great battle outside of Haugesund to honor King Harald, as the greatest early king of Norway. It is believed to be on the site where his burial mound exists.

During much of its history, fishing for herring dominated the local economy, but the stocks have been so badly depleted that they have not been viable since the early years of the 20th century. But since the mid 1960's, Haugesund, like Stavanger, has become a major center for servicing the oil drilling platforms off shore in the North Sea. Limited fishing still adds to the local economy, but nowhere near where it did a century earlier.

SIGHTSEEING DURING YOUR PORT CALL: Many cruise lines choose to bypass Haugesund, especially if they stop in Stavanger because the two cities are so close to one another. But if you are fortunate enough to visit Haugesund, it most likely will be a short port call, either a few hours in the morning or afternoon, as rarely do any cruise ships spend an entire day. Haugesund is too small to have a hop on hop off bus, but local taxi drivers will be on the dock and you can easily arrange for a short or long tour of the city and its surroundings based on a reasonable hourly rate. And the majority of the drivers do speak English. As usual, you can take a group tour around the city offered by the cruise line, but you lack the freedom to see just what is of interest to you, and stopping to photograph is limited. For those of you who want to go off on your own, here are my recommendations of places you really should see:

* Arquebus War History Museum is located at the top end of Førrestfjorden about 30 kilometers from Haugesund. This is one of those special locations that requires either a private car or taxi unless it happens to be part of a shi's tour. The museum is housed in a former German bunker, and is one of the best in Norway for telling the history of the Nazi occupation during WWII. The museum is open daily from 11 AM to 5 PM during the summer season.

* Djupadalan is an outdoor wooded area set aside for public hiking and recreation. If you are an outdoor type and would like to spend a few hours trekking through the woods on a well-marked path, this is the place to visit. It is located about eight kilometers east of the town center in the foothills and can be reached by private car or local taxi. This is a delightful walk that is suitable for all ages, and bicyclists often use this route, with bicycle rentals available in the city center.

* Haraldshaugen - This is the most recognized major site to visit within Haugesund. It is located just north of the city and can be reached by private car or local taxi. You can also walk, as it is only two kilometers from the city center. Built in 1872, it commemorates the 1,000th anniversary of the famous battle fought in this area that ultimately unified southern Norway under the Viking King Harald Fairhair. He is also believed to be buried here according to the Norwegian Sagas.

* Haraldsgata is the main pedestrian shopping street, and it gives you a good look at the basic lifestyle of the city
Our Savior's Church dominates the skyline of the city center with its tall, red tower. The architectural style is very typical of 18th or 19th century churches in small Norwegian cities. And the landscaped grounds surrounding the church offer a quiet refuge

*Haugesund Town Hall is one of the most beautiful public buildings along the southern coast of Norway. Given as a gift by a wealthy ship owner, it only dates to 1931, yet it has become recognized as an architectural masterpiece throughout the country

* Steinsfjellet - Located about 20 kilometers east of the city at an altitude of 227 meters or 744 feet above sea level, this observation point gives you a grand view of the city, surrounding woods, small lakes and the shoreline. The drive is rather pleasant, but being outside of the city, you need to have arranged for a private car or hire a local taxi.

DINING OUT: Unless your port call is for an entire day, you will either leave before the lunch hour or arrive afterwards. But for those who can spend an entire day in Haugesund, or for those who want a quick snack, I am providing my recommendations for two traditional Norwegian restaurants and one cafe that offers light snacks.

* **Brasserie Brakstad** - Located in the city center at Kaigata #2 and open from 11 AM to MIDNIGHT Monday thru Thursday, remaining open to 1:30 AM Friday and Saturday. Sunday hours are from NOON to 11 PM. this restaurant offers a casual atmosphere. The menu features a wide variety of Norwegian and general Scandinavian dishes featuring both seafood and meat entrees.

Lothus Mat & Vinhus - On the city waterfront at Skippergata # 4, this is a very popular local establishment featuring traditional Norwegian cuisine, which includes many seafood dishes. Many patrons consider it to be the best restaurant in the city. Hours are from 11 AM to 11 PM Monday thru Thursday, 11 AM to 1:30 AM Friday and Saturday and closed on Sunday.

* **Naturbaskt** - Located at Haraldsgata and Skippergaten, and open from & AM onward, this is an ideal bakery/cafe where you can get a variety of sandwiches, soups and typical Norwegian pastries. This is my recommendation for a cafe that offers quick service and light meals. They are open from 7 AM to 6 PM Monday thru Friday, closing at 4 PM Saturday. On Sunday they do not open until 9 AM and close at 4 PM.

SHOPPING: As in Stavanger, there are a few small shops selling tourist souvenirs, but the remainder of shops cater to local needs. If you are looking to invest in knitted sweaters or other local crafts, you will find the largest selection in Bergen.

FINAL WORDS: If you visit Haugesund and you are fortunate enough to have clear, sunny weather, you will find this a delightful community. But as noted earlier, weather plays a major role and when it is foggy there is less likelihood that you will dock if scheduled to do so. But when you are able to visit, Haugesund, though nothing special, is just an enjoyable place in which to savor a bit of small city life Norwegian style.

THE HEART OF HAUGESUND

The city center of Haugesund

This map is best viewed directly from OpenStreetMap.com on your personal device where it can be expanded or one specific area can be enlarged. Given the format of this book, it is impossible to display maps with the level of detail you might wish to have while actually out exploring the city. But the OpenStreetMap maps used directly are the tool I always rely upon.

Flying over Haugesund, (Work of Haugesund Avis Aerophoto)

Looking north along the main water channel through central Haugesund

Looking south along the main channel through Haugesund

Sunday summer crowds along the downtown waterfront

Strandgata is the main shopping street of Haugesund

Strandgata is very lively on a summer Sunday

Our Savior's Cathedral in the heart of Haugesund

Typical white painted wood houses of Haugesund

Haraldshaugen monument to early Viking history stands outside of town

An oil drilling platform being built in Haugesund

BERGEN
NORWAY'S SECOND CITY

Map of Greater Bergen (© OpenStreetMap contributors)

Bergen is the second largest city in Norway and for many cruise itineraries through the fjord country, it is the largest city that the ship will visit since few such cruises begin or end in Oslo. Today Bergen's population, including all of its outlying suburban reaches, is approximately 420,000. The city does not seem that large because of its physical geography. The first map in this chapter makes it easy to understand how the perception of size is affected by the urban layout. The city center is found on a small peninsula formed by two deep-water inlets, giving the city two distinct harbors. Mt. Fløyen rises up to the north of the main harbor, reaching a maximum elevation of 987 meters or 3,238 feet. The bulk of the urbanized zone stretches from the city center southward in a narrow valley that is formed between two parallel mountain ridges. In the south it reaches another deep-water inlet, extending to the international airport. There are also urbanized areas along the northern shore underneath Mt. Fløyen and extending around the northern and western edge of the mountains to the south of the central peninsula. Suburbs also spill out onto the large islands that protect the city from the full force of North Sea winters. A series of bridges connect the main islands to the heart of the city and for the smaller urbanized islands there is a fleet of small ferryboats. Bergen is so broken into small urban zones by its physical geography that it is very difficult to appreciate just how large the city is. The impression visitors receive is that of a moderate size city.

This complex geographic interrelationship between land and water is again the result of glacial scour. Numerous tongues of glacial ice swept down former river valleys between the mountain spurs and their forward edges coalesced when they reached the sea, which at that time was much lower than today. After retreating the sea rose and it flooded these now deepened channels, creating the complex network of fjords and islands. The deep channels between the mainland and those pieces of land that now form the complex strings of islands along Norway's coast present a unique urban landscape where each neighborhood appears to be a village or town in its own right. Many small scoured basins amid the mountains filled with melt water and today comprise the thousands of glacial lakes that pepper the landscape.

The entire region is cloaked in thick coniferous forest, its growth heightened by the heavy precipitation that results from mild, moist air being forced to rise along the mountainous coast. This maritime climate begins to change in the vicinity of Bergen, as the more northerly latitude equates to shorter winter days, which end up being colder and thus snowfall down to sea level is more common that farther south at Stavanger. Summers are mild with daytime temperatures rarely climbing above the mid 20's Celsius or upper 70's Fahrenheit. Gray overcast and fog are commonplace, and Bergen is said to be the least sunny major city in Norway. With climatic changes, rainfall in Bergen has increased and today averages close to 2,280 millimeters or 90 inches per year. The city actually announces in its tourist brochures that it is the rainiest city in the country and chides itself in not having a sunnier climate. Thus when you visit Bergen you should not expect blue skies and sunshine, although during July and August there can be several consecutive days with absolutely beautiful weather that makes the city so amazingly photogenic. At times the temperature can climb into the mid 20's Celsius or upper 70's Fahrenheit. In my photos at the end of this chapter, I have chosen from among my best taken over the past ten years of multiple visits. Perhaps that is not fair to those of you reading this book, as it gives a false illusion of Bergen's true weather. But at least knowing is being prepared. Bring an umbrella and a raincoat, but perhaps the Viking gods will shine upon you.

BERGEN 'S HISTORY: There is a bit of rivalry between the residents of Bergen and those of Oslo. Both cities date to within a few years of one another, so they are each among the oldest cities in Norway. But Bergen was the capital and most important city of Norway during its early years as a unified nation until the year until sometime during the reign of King Hakon V who moved the capital to Oslo sometime after 1299. Thus Bergen residents take pride in their early royal history while Oslo residents take pride in the fact that their city is now the capital and also the largest city of the nation.

The Bergen Domkyrken (cathedral) was built in 1150 and was the site of royal functions such as coronations, marriages and burials all through the rest of the 12th and 13th centuries. During its latter part of its time as the early capital, the Bergenhus Fortress, which stands watch over the northern harbor, served as a royal residence. During the 14th century, despite having lost the capital to Oslo, Bergen was a minor trade center under the Hanseatic League, but the surviving architecture along the waterfront of Bryggen lacks the distinctive ornamentation of traditional Hanseatic buildings. However, their unique character and wood construction has merited UNESCO World Heritage status.

Bergen grew both as a port, but also as a major center for the catching of cod and the drying of the fish for export. The trade became so lucrative that if any other city wanted to develop its own cod fishing/drying enterprise, it first had to obtain permission of the king.

Despite its loss of the capital, Bergen was still a major Scandinavian city, and actually was larger than Oslo until almost the mid 19th century. It suffered the bubonic plague in the mid 14th century, was attacked by pirates in the 15th century and by a British naval fleet that was after a Dutch treasure fleet under city protection in 1655.

Like Oslo, Bergen also suffered from the ravages of fire because of the persistent use of wood as the primary building material. Various parts of the city experienced massive burning during every century until the mid 20th century. Today that danger still exits in Bryggen and other older neighborhoods where wood houses are clustered together along narrow streets that often are very steep where parts of the city climb the surrounding hills.

Bergen was among the first cities in Norway to be attacked and then occupied by Nazi forces during April 1940. Because of its port facilities, it became an important German naval facility and was subjected to bombing by Allied forces. Given its strategic location along the major shipping lane for the Allies in their aid of the Soviet Union, Bergen was of prime value to the German navy.

In the late 20th century the cruise industry discovered the Norwegian fjords, and ever since Bergen has been the major urban stop on almost all itineraries. During a typical summer day there can be three to four major cruise ships anchored in Bergen, generating thousands of visitors and significant revenue for the city's merchants and tour operators.

VISITING BERGEN: Most cruise passengers opt for one of the ship's tours when visiting Bergen simply because it is a large, spread out city. A tour maximizes your time and enables you to see more of the major sights. But you do not have the freedom of stopping where you want or spending as much time as you may wish in any given venue.

A less expensive, but not as good an option is the hop on hop off bus, and there is almost always one waiting in front of the cruise dock. However, when several ships are in port the hop on hop off busses can get very crowded and at times there are long lines just to board. But with this option you can alight and spend time in and around any given designated spot and then wait for the next bus. But again I caution you to remember that these busses can become quite crowded if multiple ships are in port.

There are always taxis waiting at the portside end of the cruise terminal. For an hourly fee you can arrange to tour the city or visit particular sights. It is more costly than the cruise sponsored tours or the hop on hop off bus, but far less expensive than a private car and driver. To arrange a tour in advance, you can contact *www.en.visitbergen.com.*

Of course my preferred option is to have a private car and driver when it comes to a city this size. The ship's concierge can arrange for a car and driver, but the cost is quite significant. The largest company offering this service is Viatour and you can contact their website at *www.viatour.com.*

You can explore on foot or combine walking with public transport, but it will be far more time consuming and at the end of the day you will be exhausted.

My recommendation for the must see sights in Bergen includes:

* Bergen Fish Market - Red is the color that best describes the Fish Market, located at the upper end of the north harbor, opposite Bryggen and at the start of the city's main shopping street, which is Torgallmenningen. Between the displays of fresh salmon, cooked crab and shrimp and the magnificent strawberries and raspberries, red dominates the Fish Market. Jars of primarily salmon caviar are also available and make a popular souvenir item to take home. There are vendors selling cooked or smoked fish ready to eat on the spot or hot fish soup. But most visitors come just to look and photograph the displays of seafood and berries. If you happen to see a dark reddish brown meat that looks more like fresh beef liver, it is not. It is whale meat, as Norway and Japan are two nations where whale meat is still considered a delicacy and neither country will sign onto a moratorium on whaling. At times Green Peace protestors have come to Bergen and other Norwegian ports to garner public support, but so far to no avail. The fish market opens at 8 AM and during summer it remains open until 11 PM. However, most of the action is seen during the morning hours, as the fresh fish comes in and is quickly bought by local shoppers. But at the same time, this is the most crowded time of day with regard to tourists off various cruise ships. But by evening, if your ship is remaining late, there are far fewer tourists to contend with.

* Bryggens Museum - This small museum located in the old city district of Bryggen at Dreggsallmenningen # 3 and open daily from 10 AM to 4 PM during the summer season presents a good look at life in Bergen in the days of the city's early development through the Hanseatic period.

* Historic Bryggen - Here along the waterfront you will find the oldest surviving wood buildings in the city. Bryggen was once the center of the Hanseatic merchant's quarter and dates back to the 14th and 15th century. Many of the buildings today house fine arts and crafts shops, cafes and restaurants. This is the most popular part of the city center and is often crowded when two or more ships are in port. Most of the shops and cafes in Bryggen remain open well into the evening hours.

* KODE - The Art Museum of Bergen located along the southeastern edge of Festplassen, it is a significant art museum featuring many works by famous Scandinavian artists. It is open from 11 AM to 4 PM Tuesday thru Sunday.

* Mt. Fløyen - This is the number one tourist venue on anyone's list of places to see in Bergen. But there is one caveat - The weather must be good. Mt. Fløyen is reached by a funicular whose base is opposite the famous fish market at the upper end of the north harbor. The funicular will take you up to the observation level atop the mountain, 320 meters or 1,049 feet above sea level for a very dramatic view over the entire city and its surrounding mountains, water and islands. All of Bergen will be at your feet, but only if it is a blue sky day or if scattered clouds are above the level of the surrounding mountains. If you are going on your own, I recommend as early in the day as possible because the crowds gather soon after 9 AM and the wait can be well over an hour, but it is worth the wait. If you are on a tour, your group will get special preference. There is a teahouse and gift shop along with walking trails on top of the mountain. The funicular operates from 7:30 AM to 11 PM daily. The cafe atop the mountain is open from 10 AM to 6 PM daily, but the gift shop keeps longer hours from 9 AM to 8 PM daily.

* Rosenkrantz Tower - Often called the Bergen Castle or Fortress, it was begun in 1270 but not completed until 1560. It served as both a royal residence and a watchtower because of its position on the northern harbor. It is also part of the overall fortress defenses that once protected the city. During summer the fortress opens at 6:30 AM and remains open until 11 PM.

* St. Mary's Church - This beautiful Romanesque building dates back to the 12th century when Bergen was the first capital of a united Norway. It is where early Norwegian kings had their coronations, weddings and funerals. Located at Dreggen # 15 it is easy to spot from a distance by looking for its twin bell towers. The church is open between 9 AM and 4 PM Monday thru Friday. Between June 1 and August 31 there is a guided tour offered at 3:30 PM in English.

* Troldhaugen - This is the small house and estate that was home to Norway's most celebrated classical composer, Edvard Grieg. It is a museum dedicated to the famous composer and somewhat of a shrine to those familiar with the composer's music. Open daily from 9 AM to 6 PM during summer, it is often offered as a special ship's tour on various cruise lines. If you go on your own and do not have a car, take the light rail from the city center at Festplassen and get off at Hop Station then follow the signs.

DINING OUT: Most cruise itineraries allow a full day and often many ships remain for much of the evening in Bergen. With the great variety of restaurants located in the city center, which is a short walk from where cruise ships dock, I highly recommend either lunch or dinner in the city. Here is a chance to enjoy great Norwegian food with a heavy emphasis upon fresh seafood. I have several restaurant recommendations primarily for lunch, but a few do remain open for dinner and in each case I have chosen a venue that specializes in traditional Norwegian cuisine.

* Bare Vestland is a traditional Norwegian restaurant that specializes in both seafood and meats prepared in the western Norwegian tradition. Their menu is very diverse and there will be a dish or two to please any taste, and they also have a broad selection of beers. Open Monday thru Wednesday from 4 to 10 PM for dinner, Thursday thru Saturday open from Noon to 10 PM for lunch and dinner and on Sunday from 3 to 9 PM for early dinner. They are ocated close to the Fish Market at Vaagsallmenningen #2, this is a place that many locals patronize, so it is not strictly for tourists.

* Bryggeloftet & Steuene is a major restaurant on the waterfront in Bryggen. You cannot miss it because of its large marquee at the front. It is also in a prominent multi story brick building, which is not a common sight in Bergen. Open Monday thru Saturday from 11 AM to 11:30 PM and on Sunday from 1 to 11:30 PM. You will find a very diverse menu, but the emphasis is upon seafood. And one of its specialties is a delicious fish soup, a Norwegian tradition. This is a top choice for either lunch or dinner and it is only about a 15 minute walk from where most ships dock.

* Daily Pot - At Vaskerveien # 21, this is one of the most revered small restaurants with a stellar reputation. It is right in the center of the city. It is especially well known for its great soups, especially fish soup, which is such a Norwegian dish. The cuisine and service are

superb. Soup and salad are the specialties and many dishes are fit for vegan tastes. They are open Monday thru Friday from 11 AM to 8 PM and on weekends from Noon to 8 PM.

* Fjellskal Fisketorget - Located on the waterfront just to the south and west of the Fish Market at Strandkalen #3, this is one of the city's most noted seafood restaurants. Opening at 8 AM, it remains open way into the night, serving both lunch and dinner. The array of fish and shellfish dishes is quite amazing, as are the fish soups. Freshness is the hallmark along with excellent preparation. And you are directly on the water where fishing boats are docking to unload their catch.

* Klosterette Kaffebar- This casual restaurant is located near the heart of the city at Klosterette # 16 just off of Haugeveien, a short walk from the main square. It is easy to reach on the hop on hop off bus at stop # 5. It is noted for its excellent soups, especially the traditional fish soup. Fish cakes are a popular dish, but they also surprisingly do make a good burger for those who want something heartier. This is definitely a local cafe but one that does welcome the occasional tourist. Their hours are from 10 AM to 8:30 PM Monday thru Thursday, remaining open to 9 PM Friday. Weekend hours are from 11 AM to 9 PM.

* Krok og Krinkle Bokcafe - If dessert is all you crave, this is the place to come, as it is considered the number one cafe for typical Norwegian pastries. Located at Lille Oevregaten # 14 just uphill from the Fish Market and open from 9 AM to 7 PM, you can enjoy a light breakfast, coffee or pastry in a relaxed atmosphere among shelves of books and antique furniture pieces. It is the type of cafe where people choose to linger.

* Restaurant Cornelius - If you want to escape the city and the hordes of tourists, have the ship make a lunch or dinner reservation at this restaurant located on the island of Byorøya south of the city center in the main fjord along which the city is built. You will be given instructions as to where to meet their private boat that will take you to the restaurant and return you to the city. Here you will enjoy a fantastic seafood dinner pared with great wines in a setting that is idyllic and if the weather is nice, you can eat outside on their deck overlooking the water. They open at noon daily, but a reservation is necessary since they must arrange transportation.

SHOPPING: As a major city and also a center for tourism, there are many good shopping venues in Bergen, but only one that I felt was significant in its uniqueness. In addition, I note the downtown mall, but it does not measure up to what you would find in Oslo or other major Scandinavian cities. There are many small shops in Bryggen that sell the typical souvenirs and also the hand knitted Norwegian sweaters. But frankly none stand out as very unique. And you will find the same types of gift items, sweaters and kitsch all throughout your cruise. It is just that Bergen has a larger selection and better prices.

* Galleriet - This is the largest shopping mall in the city center, located at Torgallmenningen # 8 in the heart of the downtown. It contains a variety of shops and cafes on several levels, but it is nothing out of the ordinary if you have previously shopped in other major cities. But it does offer all of the basics, and when it comes to men's and women's casual clothing there are several Norwegian brands that are of good quality at reasonable prices. The mall is open weekdays from 9 AM to 9 PM and Saturday from 9 AM to 6 PM. And the mall is closed on Sunday.

* Julehuset Christmas Shop is a place where you can celebrate Christmas all year. It is located in Bryggen at Holmedalsgaarden #1 and open from 10 AM to 8 PM daily. On three floors you will find a wide array of souvenir items along with traditional Norwegian Christmas decorations and tree ornaments.
*

FINAL COMMENTS: Over the years that I have traveled through Norway, I have been to Bergen at least a dozen times. I always enjoy the overall flavor of the city, appreciating its antiquity mixed with modernity. It is exceptionally fresh and clean and has essentially an unhurried feeling even though thousands of tourists crowd into Bryggen and the Fish Market area. But you can take many quiet walks through its older residential areas, or ride the light rail out to quiet, leafy suburbs and come to understand what it is like to live in this coastal city. The only real drawback can be the weather, which is so hard to predict. One never knows if it will be a rainy day, just overcast or if you will have blue skies. In July and August you will find the greatest chance of experiencing nice weather in Bergen, which unfortunately is the norm rather than the exception. But please do not let the weather limit your getting out and experiencing the city. Umbrellas should always be at hand.

MAPS OF BERGEN

THE INNER REACHES OF BERGEN

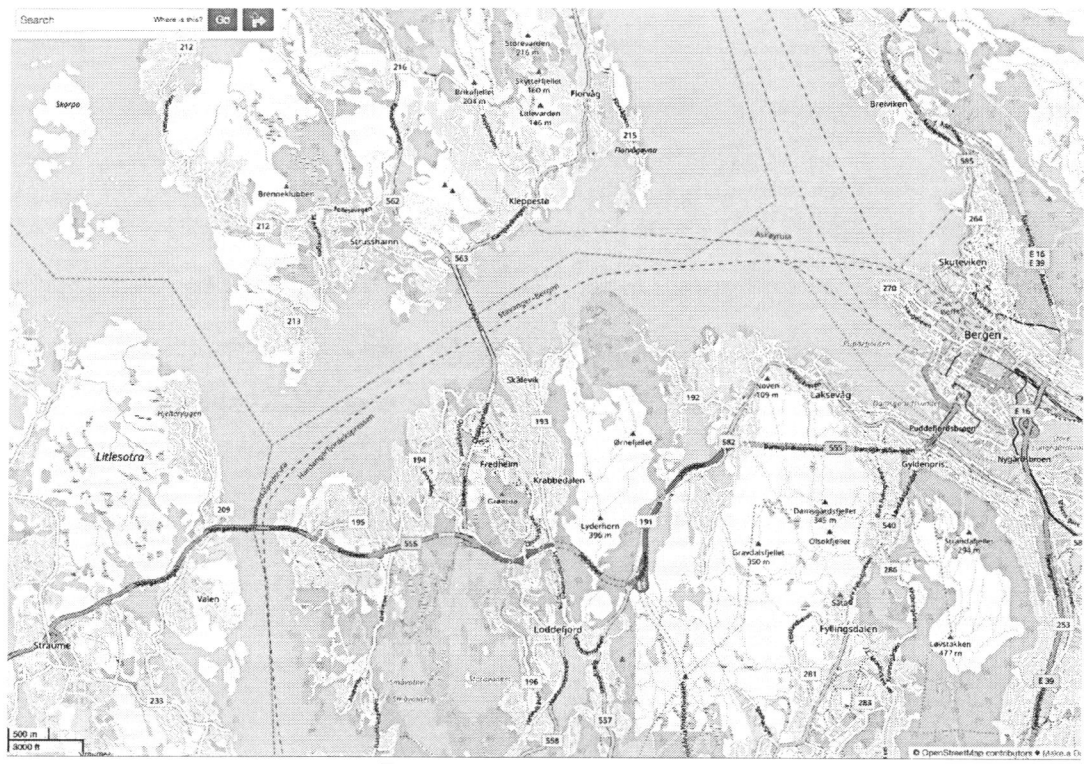

Inner reaches of Bergen

This map is best viewed directly from OpenStreetMap.com on your personal device where it can be expanded or one specific area can be enlarged. Given the format of this book, it is impossible to display maps with the level of detail you might wish to have while actually out exploring the city. But the OpenStreetMap maps used directly are the tool I always rely upon.

THE MAIN PENINSULA OF BERGEN

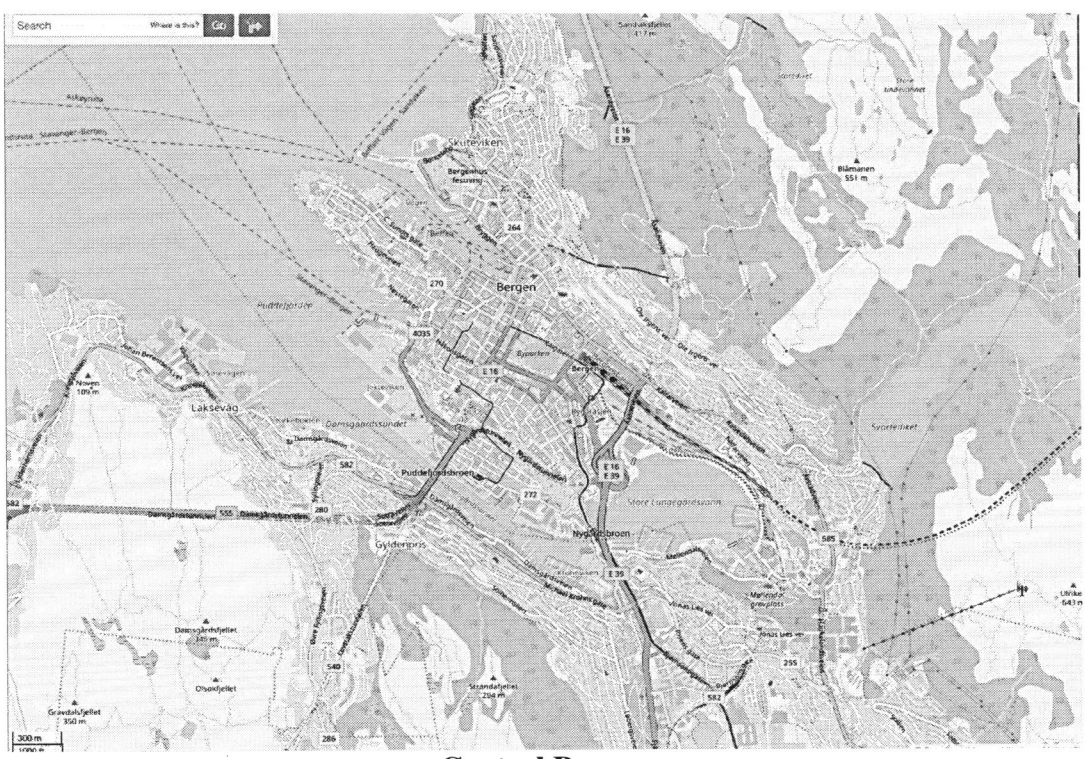

Central Bergen

This map is best viewed directly from OpenStreetMap.com on your personal device where it can be expanded or one specific area can be enlarged. Given the format of this book, it is impossible to display maps with the level of detail you might wish to have while actually out exploring the city. But the OpenStreetMap maps used directly are the tool I always rely upon.

THE HEART OF BERGEN

The heart of Bergen

This map is best viewed directly from OpenStreetMap.com on your personal device where it can be expanded or one specific area can be enlarged. Given the format of this book, it is impossible to display maps with the level of detail you might wish to have while actually out exploring the city. But the OpenStreetMap maps used directly are the tool I always rely upon.

THE VERY CENTER OF BERGEN

The very center of Bergen

This map is best viewed directly from OpenStreetMap.com on your personal device where it can be expanded or one specific area can be enlarged. Given the format of this book, it is impossible to display maps with the level of detail you might wish to have while actually out exploring the city. But the OpenStreetMap maps used directly are the tool I always rely upon.

Sailing amid the islands to reach Bergen

A view from Mt. Fløyen looking over central Bergen

A view from Mt. Fløyen looking to the left of the view above

A third view from Mt. Fløyen still farther to the left of the view above

The main waterfront behind the fish market in central Bergen

Bryggen along the waterfront, heart of old Bergen

Some of Bryggen's old buildings opposite fish market

In the amazing Bergen fish market

The ready to eat meals in the fish market

Fresh summer berries found in the fish market

The main square in the central part of Bergen

On Ole Bulls Plass in the central city

The lake in the center of Festparken is a gathering place

Feeding pigeons in the heart of Festparken

The Festparken gazebo is a focal point for gathering

The Festparken gazebo is a central city landmark

Old parts of Bergen climb the sides of Mt. Fløyen

Much of residential Bergen consists of white wood houses with red roofs

The light rail line connects the newer outer suburbs to the south

SOGNEFJORD
VISITING FLÄM AND GUDVANGEN

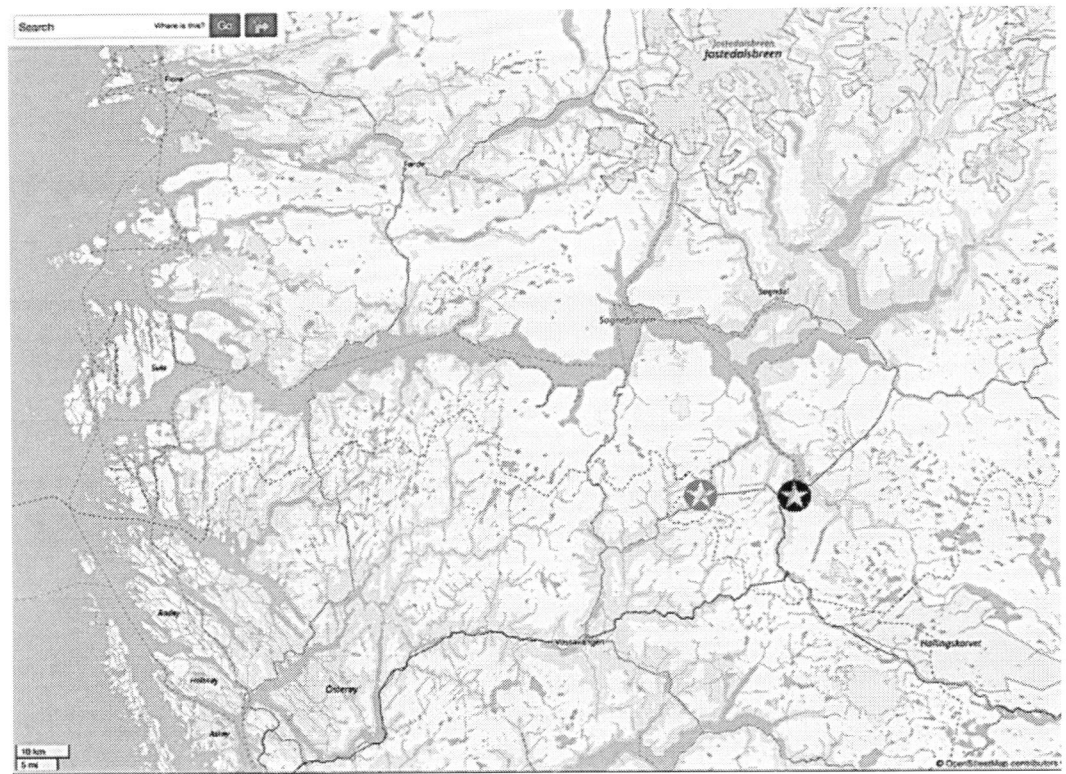

Sognefjord country, Fläm is the right hand star, Gudvangen the left hand star, (© OpenStreetMap contributors)

Visiting Fläm and Gudvangen is often the highlight of those cruises that are not going all the way north into Arctic Norway. It is very difficult to say which fjord system is the most beautiful. I have my favorites based upon their photogenic attributes, but in essence every fjord in Norway is special. And the Sognefjord system with its two major stops of Fläm and Gudvangen is hard to duplicate. Depending upon the amount of cloud cover vs. sunlight, the dappling of the landscape while sailing into these two small villages can simply be magical. There is no other word that seems to describe it. In all my years of visiting these two destinations, no two visits have ever been the same. The moods and shadows versus the brilliance of sunlight is everchanging.

Remember that fjords are the result of pre glacial river systems having been scoured by glacial ice, often widened and definitely deepened most often with sheer vertical walls. Every major fjord thus has tributary smaller fjords, presenting a rather complex landscape that can extend over 100 kilometers from the upper reaches to the sea. In the days before glaciation tiny creeks converged together and then formed the major pre glacial river system. Today they plunge directly down into the now deepened gorges, creating what amounts to hundreds of waterfalls. And given Norway's northern latitude and the altitude of its mountains, small glaciers still exist in the highest peaks and snow lingers along the tops of the fjords well into the summer, thus providing for sufficient water to keep the falls in full form.

The larger streams that were tributary to the main river were also gouged and deepened and today represent the branches of the overall fjord system. The two major southern branches of Sognefjord are Aurlandsfjorden, which is the location for the village of Fläm and Nærøyfjorden, home to the village of Gudvangen.

THE PORT OF FLÄM: Normally most cruise itineraries call for an early morning entry into Sognefjord, cruising slowly inbound for at least three to four hours before reaching Aurlandsfjorden, which is rather of short length. The journey is quite spectacular in the early morning light, of course providing the weather is relatively good. The best conditions are those when the sky is clear and there is a small amount of ground fog or mist swirling around the steep cliffs. I find that most often you can count the number of guests out on deck on one hand, as the majority are either sleeping or preparing for the day's activities. To experience the beauties of Sognefjord, one must normally be out on deck at around 5:30 AM. But there is still an opportunity to enjoy a different perspective during the evening sail out from Gudvangen, as most ships will not reach the open sea until approximately 10 PM.

Arrival at Fläm is generally in the morning at around 8 or 9 AM. There is a single small dock that is capable of handling one medium size cruise ship, and it is available on a first come basis whenever the local car ferries are not arriving at the same time. Despite their smaller size, for obvious reasons the car ferries take precedence over a cruise ship. In the event the dock is occupied by a ferry or an earlier ship, your ship will drop anchor in the fjord and you will tender to and from shore by means of one of the ship's lifeboats. The only disadvantage is that such transfers can add up to half an hour to the time going to or coming from shore.

Fläm is the coastal terminus of the Flämsbana, a railroad link of approximately 20.2 kilometers or 12.6 miles, but rising 867 meters or 2,844 feet in elevation. It connects Aurlansfjorden with the main railway line that links Oslo with Bergen. This train journey, which takes a little more than an hour each way, is the highlight of the day for most guests. It is one of the world's most spectacular rail journeys with a constantly changing panorama of the glacial valley, mountain peaks and a myriad of waterfalls. To accomplish the construction, the line is a single track standard gauge with corresponding overhead electric cables to provide power. There are 18 tunnels on the line, which has an average 2.8 percent grade.

Depending upon your cruise line's various options, you can either ride the train all the way to Myrdal where it connects with the main line and then return, a total journey time of approximately two hours. Some cruise lines offer a stop at Vatnahalsen where you have an hour before taking the return train. And most stops include waffles and coffee at the Vatnahalsen Inn. The longest option offered by some cruise itineraries has guests transferring to the main line train destined for Voss, located a short distance to the west. At Voss, guests board a motor coach for a dramatic journey back down the mountains, but to Gudvangen where they meet the ship later in the afternoon. And this option includes a lunch break along with many scenic stops.

For those who remain in Fläm, usually only a handful of guests, there is very little to do. Fläm is a village with a few shops, a nice hotel and a several private residences. There are a few walking paths, but the time will pass slowly since the stop is around four hours duration and after an hour there will be nothing more to see or do. Thus the most effective use of your time is to take one of the rail journey options. I can be bold enough to say that it should be an absolute must, as it is a journey of a lifetime with regard to the beauty you will see.

THE PORT OF GUDVANGEN: It will take your ship about two hours to sail back down Aurlandsfjorden and into Nærøyfjorden and the small village of Gudvangen. This is accomplished at midday, and on those days when it is sunny or even just partly cloudy, the voyage is nothing less than spectacular. Most guests will crowd into the ship's observation lounges or be out on deck to absorb the raw beauty of this transfer between the two fjords. I have done this trip at least a dozen times, and each time is like the first. I have also taken the rail-coach journey, meeting the ship in Gudvangen. Both options offer incredible vistas. On the shipboard journey the sheer walls of the two fjords, the small villages and farms tucked into every available shelf of land and the lacy ribbons of water flowing over the cliffs combine to say to you, "This is Norway at its Best."

Gudvangen is a small village located at the top end of Nærøyfjorden. It is essentially a residential village, but where car ferries dock, there is a nice visitor's center with a gift shop. And there are a few small hotels that cater to those who are traveling through the fjord country either by car, utilizing the combination of roads and ferryboat connections or the more physically active who are hiking, walking or cycling their way around the country.

The earliest hotel to open in Gudvangen was in 1830. Gudvangen is also connected directly to Fläm by way of the Gudvangen Tunnel that cuts through the mountain separating the two fjords. This has reduced the travel time by road by nearly two thirds.

In Gudvangen the dock is not large enough to accommodate any size cruise ship, thus it becomes necessary to anchor off shore and tender guests to the dock. Once in Gudvangen there is not much to do other than walk around the town and enjoy both its traditional wood architecture and the towering cliffs that surround it. The village is literally surrounded by waterfalls, a sight that is sure to please any camera enthusiast.

Gudvangen dates back to Viking times, and it has been a gathering place and small market center for approximately 1,000 years. Today there is a Viking festival held each year in late July or early August on the meadow located across the small river just east of the town. Locals dressed in traditional garb camp here in Viking fashion, performing traditional tasks, playing musical instruments and preparing food in the manner of their distant ancestors. There is a small admission fee, but this also entitles you to photograph the participants at your leisure if you are fortunate enough that your port call is during the time of the festival.

DINING OUT: Your time ashore in both Fläm and Gudvangen is so limited that there is no chance to sit and have a nice lunch. But you can have morning coffee with a pastry at the hotel in Fläm if you are not doing one of the rail journeys. If you do have any time for lunch, which is doubtful, I do recommend the main hotel dining room. The food is quite good as is the service. But generally ships stay for just a few hours and then go on to Gudvangen.

MEMORIES: Every time I have visited both Fläm and Gudvangen I have found it to be a day filled with incredible, but ever changing scenery. The mood of the landscape will depend upon the weather, but even in the worst case scenario where it rains, there is still an aura of environmental magic to the entire length of Sognefjord. Even on days when the weather is less than perfect, the fjord takes on a mood of its own that can be quite dramatic.

I do highly advise everyone to spend as much time out on deck, or if it is too cold then spend time in the observation lounge.

AURLANDSFJORDEN AND NÆRØYFJORDEN

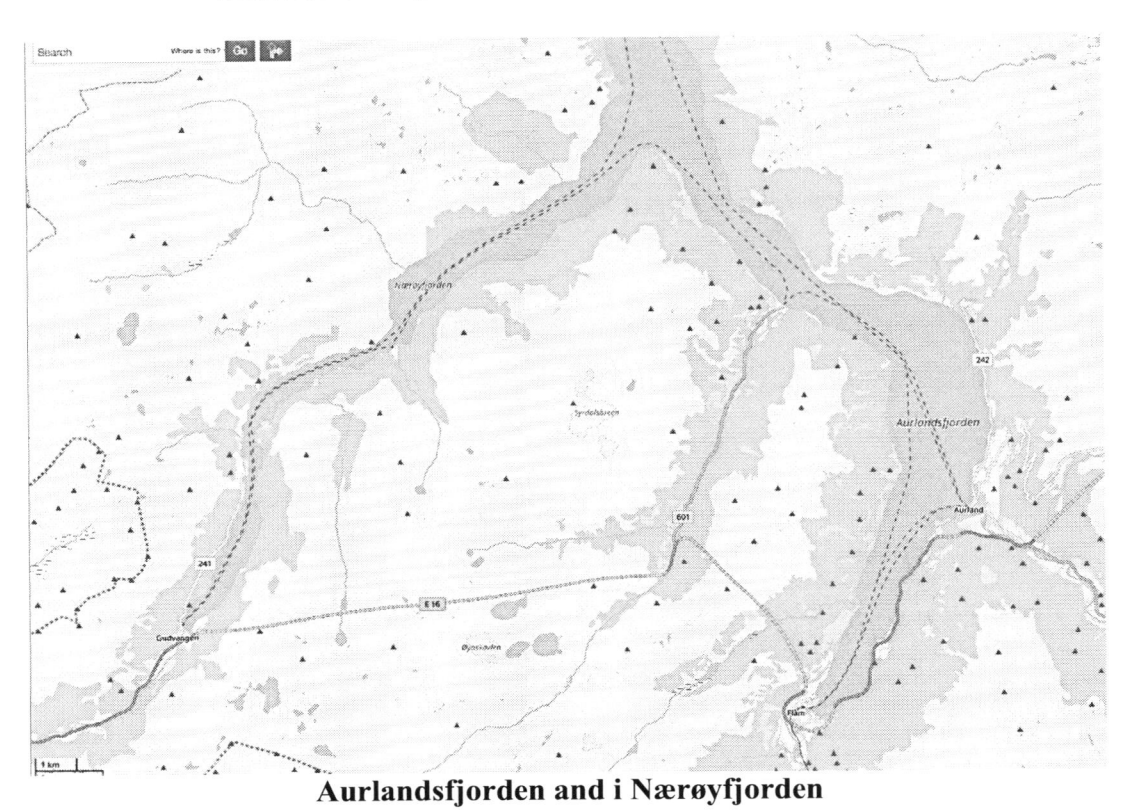

Aurlandsfjorden and i Nærøyfjorden

This map is best viewed directly from OpenStreetMap.com on your personal device where it can be expanded or one specific area can be enlarged. Given the format of this book, it is impossible to display maps with the level of detail you might wish to have while actually out exploring the city. But the OpenStreetMap maps used directly are the tool I always rely upon.

THE VILLAGE OF FLÅM

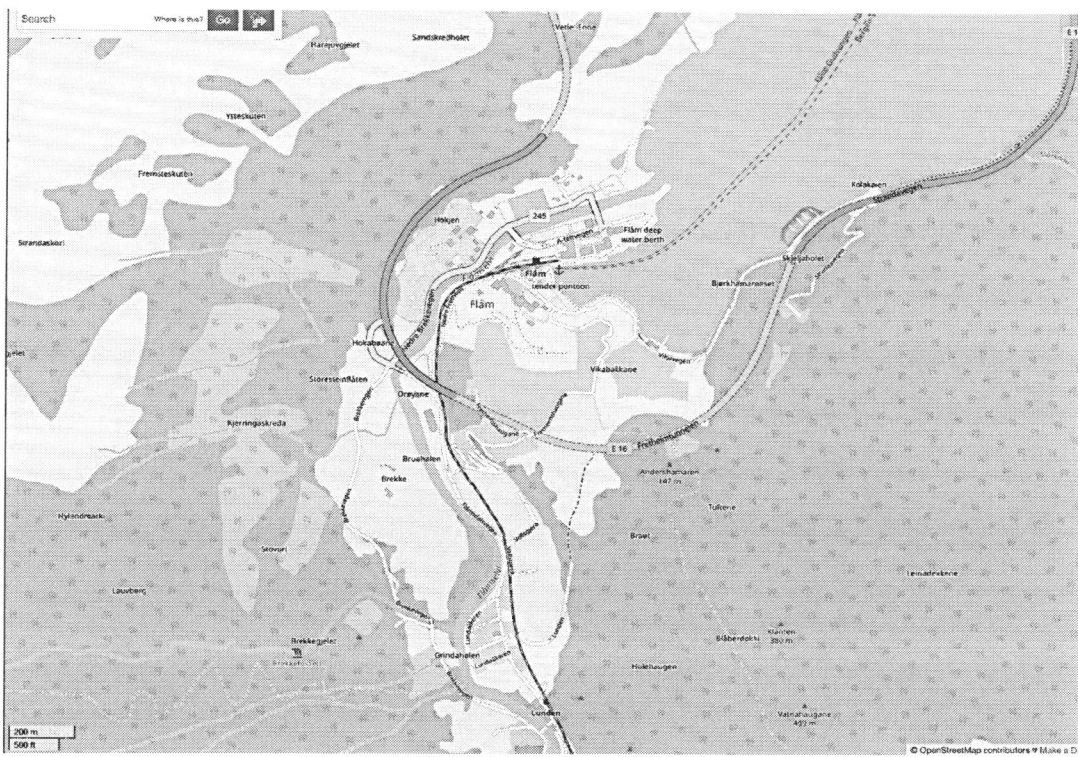

The village of Flåm

This map is best viewed directly from OpenStreetMap.com on your personal device where it can be expanded or one specific area can be enlarged. Given the format of this book, it is impossible to display maps with the level of detail you might wish to have while actually out exploring the city. But the OpenStreetMap maps used directly are the tool I always rely upon.

Sognefjorden in the early morning

Sofnefjorden and Aurlandssfjorden join

Aurlandsfjorden at the village of Undredal

The majesty of Aurlandsfjorden

The village of Fläm

The hotel in Fläm

The Flämsbana ready for departure

Heading up on the Flämsbana out of Fläm

one of the spectacular waterfalls of the Flämsbana route

Nærøyfjorden is very majestic in midafternoon light

Approaching Gudvangen

There is a quiet charm to the village of Gudvangen

The Viking festival in Gudvangen

The Viking camp is quite special if you are there at the right time

One of the many waterfalls surrounding Gudvangen

NORDFJORDEN
VISITING OLDEN

The Nordfjorden system and the location of Olden as per the star(© OpenStreetMap contributors)

Visting Olden after having sailed through the Sognefjord system the prior day (if you are sailing northbound) is almost reaching for sensory overload. Just when you thought you had seen some of the most beautiful scenery Norway has to offer, the next day you are waking up to a majestic landscape that rivals what you had just seen. If your itinerary is one in which you visit the Norfjorden system first and then sail on the following day to Fläm and Gudvangen, the same condition will apply. Which fjord system is more majestic? The answer to that question is purely subjective and a matter of taste. As one who has made the journey many times, I cannot give a definitive answer. Although I must say that the village of Olden and the chain of lakes south to the head of the Jostedalsbreen Ice Sheet is one of the most stunning landscapes in the country. And if you happen to visit on a day with dappled light, that is a mix of sun and cloud, you will experience the true glory of Norway.

Norfjorden is among the longer fjord systems in Norway, its total length being just over 106 kilometers or 63 miles. Most of its runoff comes from the large Jostedalsbreen Ice Sheet, which some maps refer to as a glacier, through four small tributary fjords that come together to form the primary Norfjord. Jostedalsbreen is the largest single mass of ancient glacial ice on the European continent, exceeded in size only by the large ice sheets of Iceland, which is a European country culturally, but not a part of mainland Europe geologically. The village of Olden is located where the rushing waters of the Oldelva River flows into Faleidfjorden,

a small extension or arm of the larger Norfjorden. The glacial melt comes from the Birksdalsbreen Glacier, which is a tongue of the larger Jostedalsbreen Ice Sheet. The glacier is located approximately 40 kilometers or 24 miles south of Olden, at the top end of the valley carved initially by the glacier thousands of years ago, and today fed by the Oldelva River.

Because of the depth of glacial scour, these fjords are especially deep, here where Faleidfjorden flows into Norfjorden it is 565 meters or 1,854 feet deep. There is no ship in the world that would have any difficulty navigating in water this deep, however, the largest cruise ships cannot be accommodated with docking facilities and the town of Olden cannot handle thousands of ship guests at one time. So the limiting factor in whether your itinerary includes a stop in Olden is not determined by the act of navigation, but rather by the inability of small villages to service the needs of large numbers of visitors at the same time. Thus if you truly want to enjoy cruising through most of the fjords of Norway, you are best off in choosing a ship that carries 500 passengers or less.

VISITING OLDEN: It takes around four hours to sail all the way through Norfjorden to the village of Olden. There is a single dock, and given that this is not a major cruise destination, it is doubtful that more than one cruise ship will be in port at a given time. Being able to dock does make the visit easier, as you do not need to spend time waiting for and then riding the tender boat to or from shore.

The Olden area is surprisingly old with regard to settlement. Evidence shows that pre Viking settlement can be traced back to the Iron Age. But the actual village of Olden is relatively young by Norwegian standards with settlement dating back to the mid 1600's, but there were scattered households at the top end of the fjord as far back as the early 1300's. The old church located in the heart of the village was built in 1759, but on the same site there was once an old stave church built back in the 1300's.

Within the Olden region, back in 1905 and again in 1936, there was a massive avalanche of rock that toppled off of Mt. Ramnefjelt into Lovatnet Lake, creating a massive series of tsunami waves that killed 102 people in the two disasters combined. This to date is the largest loss of life from any natural catastrophe in the history of Norway. Some cruise operators do offer a hike to Lovatnet Lake, not with the past disaster in mind, but for guests to simply enjoy the breathtaking scenery.

Although the village of Olden only has a resident population of 500, it is becoming more oriented to the cruise industry. There are a few local tour operators and a hop on hop off bus that meet the ship and offer affordable tours through the town and to the front of the Birksdalsbreen Glacier. And most cruise lines also offer one or more scenic tours. Apart from some cruise lines having a hike to Lovatnet Lake, most offer a coach tour to visit the Birksdalsbreen Glacier. These tours do involve a bit of hiking in order to reach viewpoints that are advantageous in seeing the glacier. And some cruise operators offer a longer coach tour to visit the more massive Jostedalsbreen Ice Sheet. Visiting Olden is all about the natural landscape, as the village itself offers only the old church and its lovely houses, sights that can be enjoyed in a matter of minutes.

DINING OUT: Olden is such a small village, and choice is very limited. Lunch is possible if you do not go on a group tour, but the majority of guests generally return to the ship given the meager selection of restaurants.

* Molla Gjesthus - Located opposite where the ship docks, is a small guesthouse with limited offerings of food and drink. It is very expensive, but it does provide local color and has a friendly staff. However, if you research the guest house on Trip Advisor you will find the reviews to be quite mixed. I personally found lunch to be quite acceptable. No actual hours are posted, but the make certain to be open when a ship is in port.

* Yris Kafe - Located in the heart of Olden, and often showing up in guide books as Per's Cafe, this small establishment offers light lunches and the prices are reasonable by Norwegian standards. It is open from 11 AM to 10 PM Monday thru Saturday and from Noon to 10 PM on Sunday.

FINAL WORDS: Again I find it hard to put into words how magnificent the scenery is when visiting Olden. The sail into this tiny village and the sail back out in the late afternoon can provide some of the most incredible photographic opportunities if there is the right mix of cloud and sun. But this being Norway, it can often be very cloudy, rainy or the fjord can be shrouded in fog. It is always a gamble.

THE VILLAGE OF OLDEN

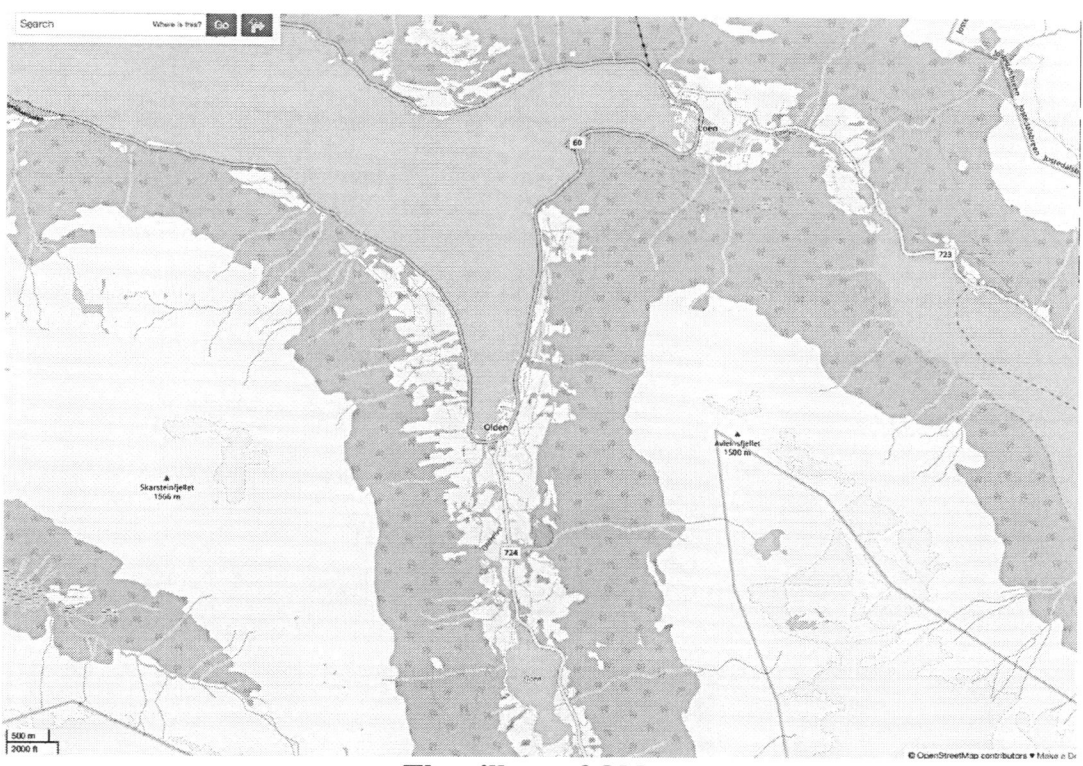

The village of Olden

This map is best viewed directly from OpenStreetMap.com on your personal device where it can be expanded or one specific area can be enlarged. Given the format of this book, it is impossible to display maps with the level of detail you might wish to have while actually out exploring the city. But the OpenStreetMap maps used directly are the tool I always rely upon.

THE OLDELVA RIVER LAKES

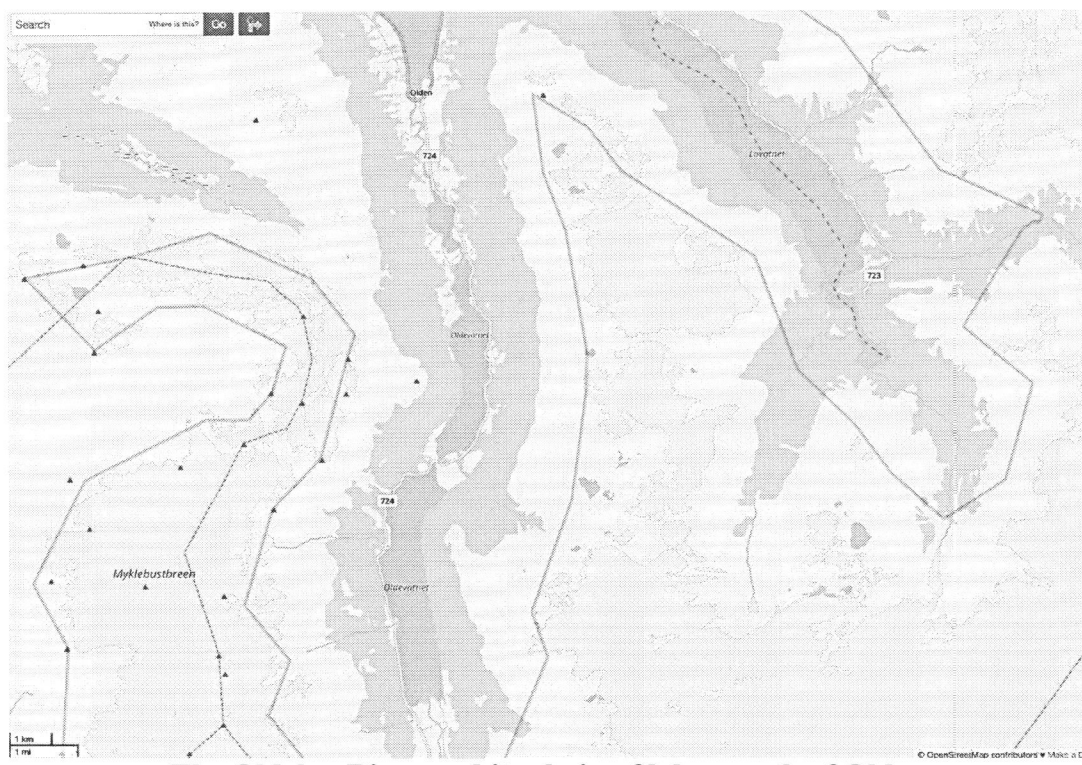

The Oldelva River and its chain of lakes south of Olden

This map is best viewed directly from OpenStreetMap.com on your personal device where it can be expanded or one specific area can be enlarged. Given the format of this book, it is impossible to display maps with the level of detail you might wish to have while actually out exploring the city. But the OpenStreetMap maps used directly are the tool I always rely upon.

Sailing up Norfjorden past the town of Loen at dawn

Along the shoreline of Norfjorden i

Sailing into Olden

First view of Olden from the ship

In the village of Olden

The old 17th century church in Olden

The fast flowing Oldelva River through Olden

The Oldelva River in whitewater south of Olden

The beauty of the lower Oldelva Lake

The magnificent beauty of Upper Lake nearest the glacier

The majesty of Upper Lakes

Sailing out from Olden in the late afternoon

ÅLESUND

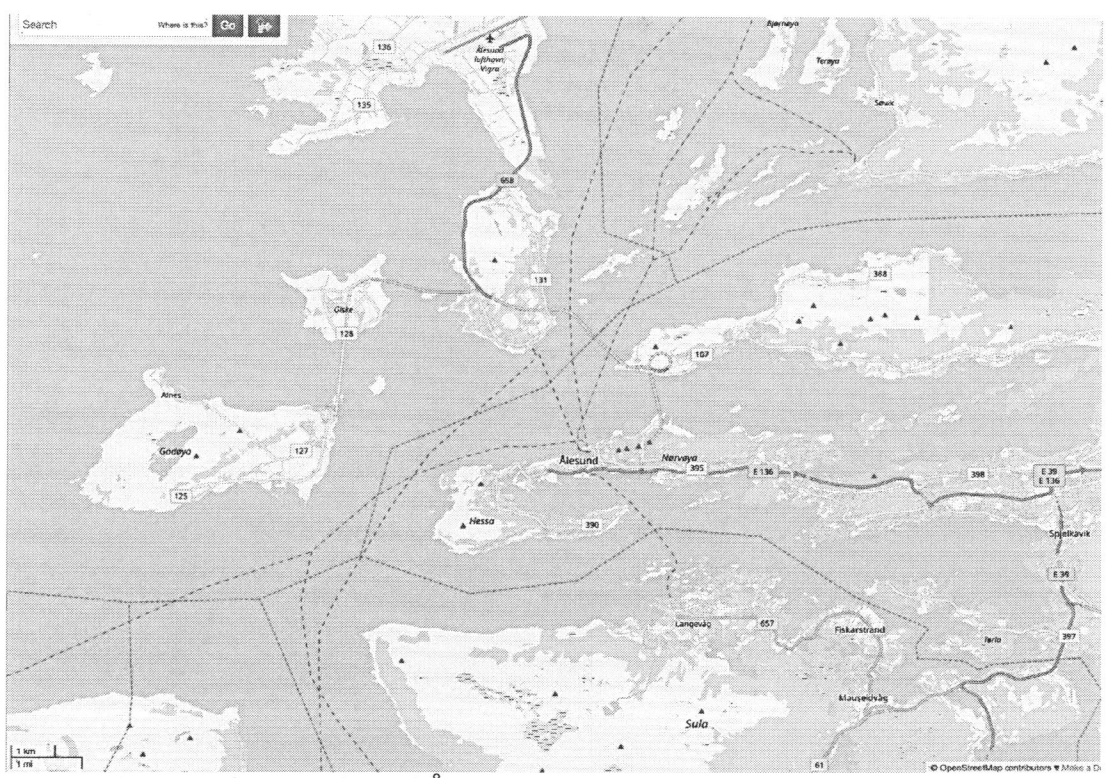

A map of the region of Ålesund (© OpenStreetMap contributors)

A visit to Ålesund comes as quite a surprise to those who are simply expecting another Norwegian town or village. Ålesund is a significant coastal city with a metro area population of approximately 49,000 residents. Both the physical setting and the architecture of the city make it quite distinctive and to some degree unique among the coastal ports of Norway.

THE PHYSICAL LANDSCAPE: Ålesund is a city of islands. It is located at a junction of several fjords that came together during the last glacial advance, carving up the landscape in such a way that when the ice melted back and sea level rose, numerous rugged offshore islands were created. Ålesund is connected by one of the channels between the islands to the entrance of Geirangerfjorden, the most visited of all of the fjords of Norway. The city actually occupies portions of seven different islands. The surrounding islands, including those that are a part of Ålesund are rocky, but not very prominent. And as is true in most of Norway below the Arctic Circle they are thickly covered in coniferous forest or woodland. The higher mountains from which the fjords originate are visible from Ålesund and their snow-covered peaks add to the overall beauty of the landscape.

The waters immediately surrounding Ålesund are calm most of the time, but can become quite choppy when the wind picks up at any time of year. Once beyond the islands, the waters of the North Sea can be quite stormy, especially in winter and often during short summer gales, making the approach to the urban area difficult at those times.

The region still falls within the maritime climate regime similar to that of Bergen and the other ports to the south. But being that the high mountains are a bit farther to the east, the rainfall totals are slightly lower and there are a few more sunny days than in Bergen, Haugesund or Stavanger because there are no significant peaks to generate rapid lifting of the moist air.

A BRIEF HISTORY: Viking legend dates back to a famous warrior in the 10th century named Rollo who came from a village just northwest of present day Ålesund, showing that the area has a long history. But the city of Ålesund itself only dates back to the early 19th century, being founded as a town in 1838. The city center of today, however, owes its unique existence to a great fire that occurred in 1904, destroying most of old primarily wooden town because of very strong winds that fanned the flames into a conflagration. Prior to the great fire, Kaiser Wilhelm of Germany used to vacation here and when he heard about this terrible fire, he sent building supplies to build shelters that would temporarily house the community. The actual rebuilding was done after initial shelter was provided, and it was decided to utilize the Art Nouveau style, which was so popular, especially in Germany. Architects and builders trained in the style were brought from Germany in to help in the rebuilding, making Ålesund a classic example today of Art Nouveau. It is so well recognized and it has an interpretative center and it is active in the Europe wide network to preserve this as an important architectural style.

What fed the Ålesund economy until the mid 1930's, was fishing, in particular for herring. But the local fishermen ultimately destroyed their bounty by devising better ways to catch the fish. By the mid 1930's, the stock became so depleted that the industry died. Today there is limited fishing, but it no longer is the mainstay of the Ålesund economy. The city has become an important regional trade center, and that is now its primary role.

During World War II Ålesund was a major hot bed for resistance, much of with close ties to the British who aided in getting many people out of the country despite the Nazi occupation. The invading military did not use Ålesund for any major activities and most allied raids were on installations farther to the north, thus sparing much damage to the architecture or infrastructure.

After the war, as Ålesund began to assume more of a regional role, new business and bank buildings in the city center led initially to the destruction of numerous of the old Art Nouveau buildings. And although they were the pride of the city, there was little to no attempt to spare them. There were even those in the community that openly welcomed the new developments as a sign that Ålesund was modernizing.

One infrastructure development that did bring total approval was the linking of the various islands within the city and beyond by means of bridges or tunnels, bringing a more cohesive transportation pattern into being. As a result, today most of the inhabited portions of Ålesund are linked together without the need for the use of ferryboats. The transport network helps to make Ålesund a major regional center with easy access to the mainland.

By the 1970's, as more demolition took place to bring in further development a backlash developed and there were demonstrations against the ongoing destruction of the city's unique architectural heritage. As a result, today Ålesund is very protective of its post 1904 fire revival, and Art Nouveau is very much a selling point in the community. The city has continued to grow and the modern development is now seen east of the city center in areas that have grown out of the former woodland and farms, and this has been welcomed, but no longer at the expense of the city center.

More cruise ships now visit Ålesund, and fortunately the main docks are right in the very heart of the city. Thus it is very easy for walking tours to be conducted or for visitors to go off on their own and explore the city center. Although most Norwegian cruises are based upon the beauty of the natural environment, there is great interest among tourists in seeing both the styles of Art Nouveau and Art Deco, as they are not that widespread in today's world.

VISITING ÅLESUND: Depending upon your cruise line, there may be several tours offered to either some of the outlying islands or to the mountainous interior, as each cruise line has its own agenda as to what they choose to provide. This section of the chapter is, however, confined to Ålesund, showing you the major sights that are capable of being seen within the urban area.

Apart from ship sponsored tours, you can easily get around the main heart of the city by walking. Local taxis are available on the dock and for a fee based upon an hourly rate, the drivers can help you explore beyond the range you can do on foot. There is a hop on hop off bus in Ålesund on a single route operating daily between 9 AM and 4 PM with eight stops. For further information visit *https://city-sightseeing.com/en/66/alesund/71/hop-on-hop-off-alesund.*

The major sights include:

* Ålesunds Museum is also in the city center, located at Rasmus Rosennebergs gate #16 and open daily between 11 AM and 3 PM daily, but closed on weekends. Allow at least an hour or more. The museum is devoted to the history of Ålesund and also to the importance of the fishing industry in the city's growth.

* Alnes Lighthouse is a very popular attraction. It is located on the outer island of Godøy, which is reached by way of a series of bridges and tunnels, showing you the way in which these settled islands are all linked to Ålesund. The ride there and back is worth the visit alone. You will need to be on a tour, providing one is offered, or you can negotiate a rate with a local taxi for the drive there and back. The modern lighthouse dates only to 1936, and its architectural style is unique in that it built with four flat, angular walls capping out at 225 meters or 738 feet in height. The lighthouse also has a small museum to help you understand its role, and it is still active in its function as a beacon for mariners. There is a cultural center adjacent to the lighthouse and a small cafe that provides refreshments and light meals.

* Atlantic Sea Park is usually the second most popular attraction, but it is not located in the city center. It is at the western end of the city via a bridge that connects central Ålesund with Hessa. It is walkable, about five kilometers or three miles, but again it is easiest to take a taxi. Again most of the tours will include a stop at the Atlantic Sea Park. The focus is the aquarium that highlights the sea life of this region, and their outdoor exhibits do include penguins even

though they are from the Southern Hemisphere and were never found in Norway. The park does put on a show with their seals, which both adults and children find very endearing. The park is open from 11 AM to 4 PM daily, and remains open to 6 PM on Sunday.

* Fjellstua Overlook is the number one visitor attraction in Ålesund, especially during clear weather. Rising up just east of the city center is the mountain known as Aksla where the Fjellstua Lodge is perched with its outdoor deck providing a dramatic view over the city and well out to sea or eastward into the fjords. You can reach the top on your own, if you have the strength to negotiate 418 steps that will climb the side of the mountain. Or you can hire a taxi to take you to the top, wait for the short time you will spend viewing the panorama and then return you to the city center. But all of the city tours that the various cruise lines offer do include a drive to the top of Aksla to enjoy the view. The viewing deck is open 24 hours per day. The Fjellstua Lodge restaurant is open Sunday thru Tuesday from 11 AM to 5 PM, Wednesday thru Saturday from 11 AM to 10 PM.

* Giske Kirke is a small regional church on the island of Giske, which is en route to the Alnes Lighthouse. The church dates to the 11th century and is well preserved, giving you a glimpse into early Christian life in Viking Norway. The church is open Monday thru Saturday from 10AM to 5 PM and on Sunday from 1 to 5 PM.

* Jugendstilsenteret and Kunstmuseet Kube is the most important museum to visit to learn about Ålesund after the 1904 fire and the development of Art Nouveau. It is just steps from where the ships dock, located at Apotekergata # 16. It is open from 11 AM to 4 PM on days when the ship is in port. This is in effect two museums for the price of one admission. A visit gives you the story of the city of Ålesund and of the Art Nouveau movement. And there is a small, but interesting museum shop. A visit then makes the architecture of the city center far more meaningful.

* Sunnmoere Museum is located a short distance east of the city and you will need to have a taxi or be on a tour to visit, but it is well worth the effort. During summer, the museum is open daily from 10 AM to 4 PM and Saturday from Noon to 4 PM with Sunday hours being from 10 AM to 4 PM. This is essentially a spacious outdoor museum that recreates Norwegian life through a number of houses and buildings along with having a display of Viking relics. The setting is very conducive to strolling about and each building presents a glimpse of life as it was. Many visitors consider this to be the best sightseeing venue in Ålesund.

This is not an exhaustive list, but presents you with the most important sights in Ålesund. But during your one day stop you must allow a couple of hours simply to wander the streets of the old inner city and soak up the architectural flavor. If your cruise does stay overnight, and if the weather is favorable, the city takes on a very beautiful glow when the sun is low in the western sky. During summer there is only a brief hour or two of darkness, but Ålesund looks so especially rich during the golden hours of late evening sun.

DINING OUT: Unless your ship should just happen to stay overnight, which is rather rare on fjord itineraries, you will be able to at least have lunch in Ålesund. Here are my recommendations for traditional Norwegian restaurants in Ålesund.

* Anno is located in the center of town at Apotekergata #9 and open from early morning to mid evening, serving all three meals. For lunch they can get rather busy, but if you come in after 1 PM, it is quiet and the service is very friendly. They are known for their fresh seafood and also pizza, but with a Norwegian twist in that you can have a salmon pizza. The combination of good, fresh food and fast service enables you to still have plenty of time for sightseeing.

* Brasserie Normandie is a relatively expensive, but high quality restaurant in the Hotel Parc Scandic located at Storgata #16. It opens at Noon and remains open until 11 PM. Their menu is diverse, but with a strong emphasis upon fresh seafood, and good desserts. Service is not rushed, sometimes even a bit slow. But the atmosphere is relaxed.

* Cafe Lyspunktet located in the city center on Kipervikgata #1 is ideal for lunch. It opens at Noon and stays open until 9 PM. They have a good menu selection including soups, sandwiches and fresh seafood dishes. Their fish soup is exceptionally good. It can become crowded at lunch, and reservations are not taken.

* Lyst Cafe Bar & Food is a very nice, traditional restaurant located in the city center on Kongens gate #12 and open from 10 to 1 AM. Again I recommend going later for lunch, as they do get rather busy. They offer a good selection of traditional and contemporary dishes with an emphasis on freshness, especially the seafood.

* Tante Bruun Cafe - Located in the city at Grimmergata # 1, this is a popular local restaurant that specializes in traditional cuisine. Soups are a popular item on the menu, but they offer a wide variety of dishes to please any taste. The restaurant is open from 10 AM to 8 PM Monday thru Saturday.

SHOPPING: There are several small souvenir stores, and also a few stores selling maritime antiques all located in the city center. But Ålesund is not a destination for any real high quality arts and crafts shopping. For that I do recommend the larger cities such as Bergen, Trondheim and Tromsø.

FINAL WORDS: I have personally always found Ålesund to be a refreshing stop. Simply wandering its streets and soaking in the unique Art Nouveau atmosphere is delightful. Local shops cater more to the needs of the residents, but there are two small shopping centers in the downtown that are interesting in that they give you a glimpse at what types of items the locals purchase. Remember that Norway has a very high living standard, but at the same time people are conservative and not motivated by conspicuous consumption. I also do recommend at least one half day tour to one of the outer islands if the weather is nice. And definitely drive or walk (if physically fit) to the top of Aksla for the incredible view, of course weather depending.

THE CITY OF ÅLESUND

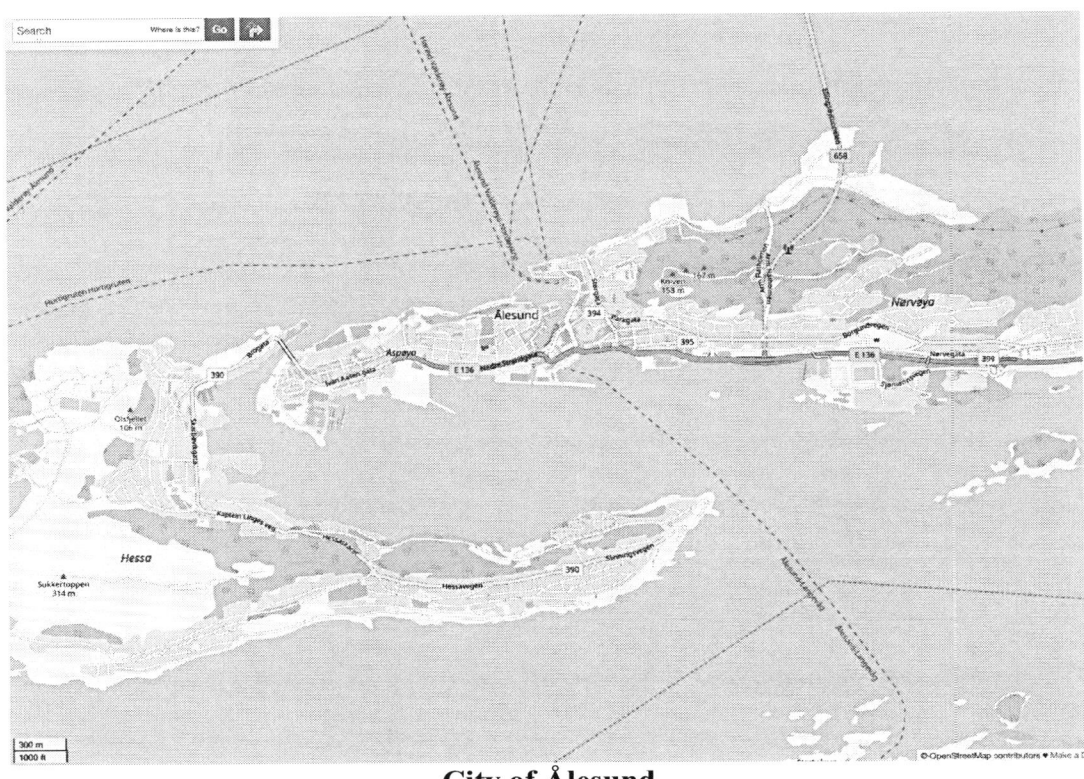

City of Ålesund

This map is best viewed directly from OpenStreetMap.com on your personal device where it can be expanded or one specific area can be enlarged. Given the format of this book, it is impossible to display maps with the level of detail you might wish to have while actually out exploring the city. But the OpenStreetMap maps used directly are the tool I always rely upon.

THE CENTER OF ÅLESUND

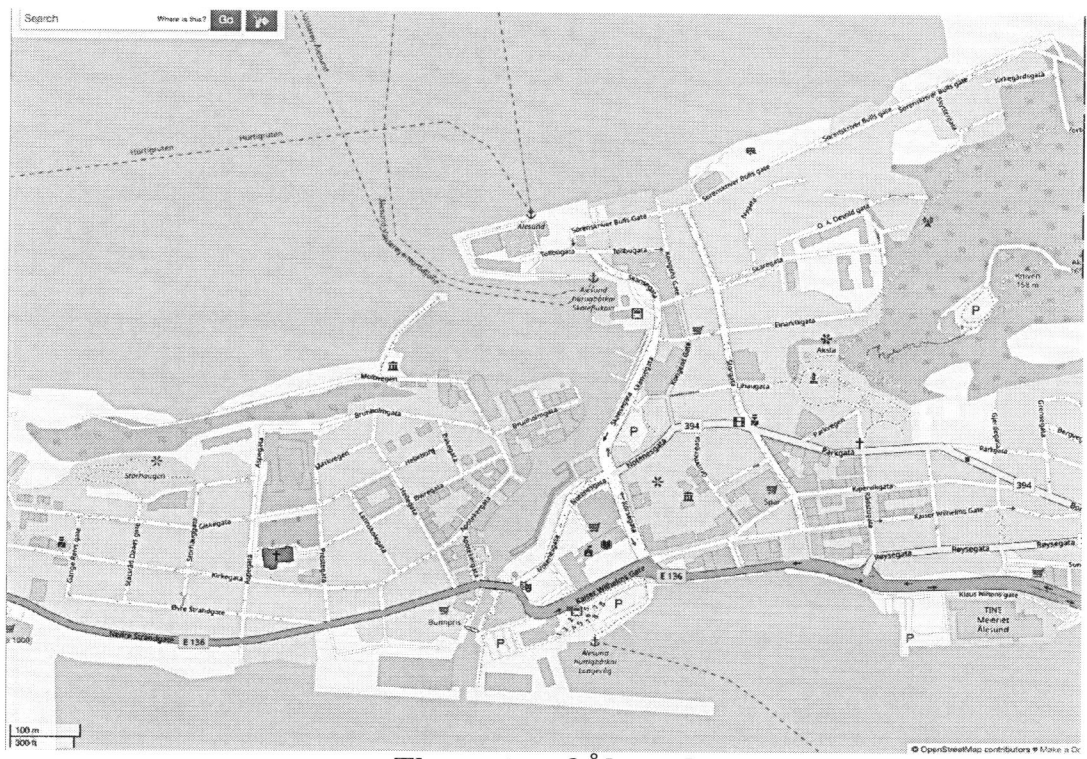

The center of Ålesund

This map is best viewed directly from OpenStreetMap.com on your personal device where it can be expanded or one specific area can be enlarged. Given the format of this book, it is impossible to display maps with the level of detail you might wish to have while actually out exploring the city. But the OpenStreetMap maps used directly are the tool I always rely upon.

Sailing into the harbor at Ålesund

The city center of Ålesund with Aksla above it

The more modern housing of Ålesund on the slopes of Aksla

Center of Ålesund from the top of Aksla

The far western side of Ålesund from Aksla

A view out to the outer islands from Aksla

Looking down on the Ålesundet from Aksla

Along the Ålesundet running through the heart of the city

Examples of Art Nouveau style along the Ålesundet

The city's main pedestrian shopping street

Maritime antiques in a downtown store window

The Sunnmøere Museum

The Alnes Lighthouse (Work of Tolpost, C, CC BY SA 3.0, Wikimedia.org)

STORFJORDEN
VISITING HELLESYLT & GEIRANGER

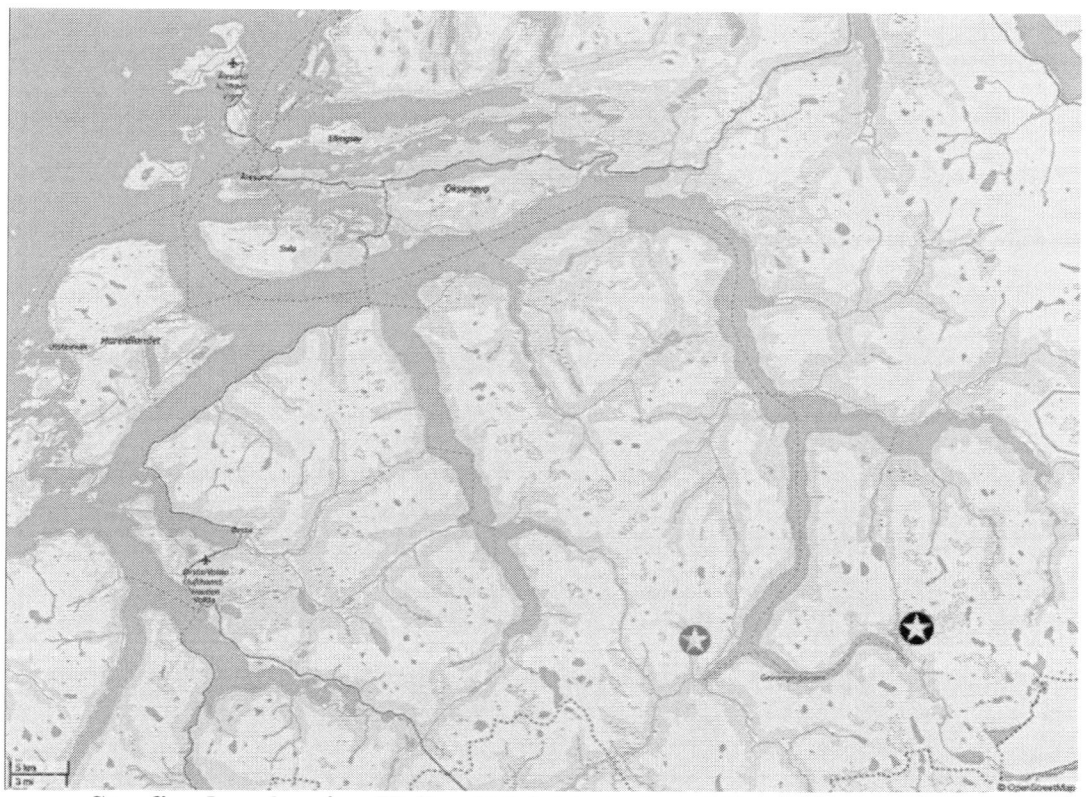

**Storfjorden showing Hellesylt (right star) and Geiranger (left star)
(© OpenStreetMap contributors)**

Every visitor to Norway comes away with his or her favorite fjord. As noted before, in reality it is difficult to say which is the more beautiful, as each has its own level of majesty and its own level of spectacular scenery. But there is a very strong favoritism shown to the Storfjorden system with its two beautiful tributary fjords of Sunnylvsfjorden (Hellesylt) and Geirangerfjorden. Many of the fjords see few if any cruise ships, but both the small ports of Hellesylt and Geiranger are especially popular destinations, and they appear on Norwegian calendars and travel posters quite regularly. It is difficult to say why these two have become the so called "poster children" for cruising the fjords of Norway other than the fact that they are the most spectacular of the southern fjord region that is reached easily on a seven-day cruise from Copenhagen or Oslo. I strongly believe this popularity developed out of proximity, as other fjords of equal or even greater magnificence lie much farther to the north of Storfjorden and thus require a longer cruise.

SAILING INTO STORFJORDEN: The distance to Hellesylt and Geiranger from the open sea requires several hours of sailing. Most cruise itineraries have the ship entering Storfjorden at around 6 AM in order to reach Hellesylt by 10 AM and Geiranger at around Noon or slightly earlier. I know most people like to sleep in during the early morning hours, especially if they attended a show or visited the casino the night before. But if you do so, you

will miss some exceptionally spectacular scenery, especially if the weather is good. And in Norway that is always the big "if" factor.

Storfjorden initially begins with lower mountains closest to the sea and the shorelines are gentle with small villages and numerous farms. As your ship proceeds inward, the mountains progressively close in, at times framing the fjord with steep cliffs that are so close that the telltale scratches created by glacial scour are visible. Waterfalls are very numerous where streams plunge down into the fjord. Once the small streams that are now high above would have merged gently with the former river system now flooded by the sea after the glaciers scoured the valleys to such tremendous depths. These waterfalls are referred to as "hanging valleys." And even if you are not particularly interested in their geologic origin, their intense beauty will mesmerize you.

HELLESYLT: By mid-morning, your ship may turn into Sunnylvsfjorden, which is a short channel that ends at the tiny village of Hellesylt. Not all cruise ships will stop here, as there are no dock facilities and the village is too tiny to host large numbers of visitors. Only those cruise ships with itineraries that offer an all-day bus tour through the mountains to rejoin the ship at Geiranger will stop and tender those guests on shore to meet their coach. For those remaining on board, with binoculars you can take a visit to this tiny village and see its thundering whitewater river that empties into Sunnylvsfjorden.

GEIRANGERFJORDEN: Most ships will proceed to enter Geirangerfjorden directly from Storfjorden, with the day's destination being the resort village of Geiranger. It will take up to 90 minutes for your ship to sail the length of Geirangerfjorden, passing between towering cliffs where numerous waterfalls are plunging into the deep waters of the fjord.

The most noted feature you will see on the port (left) side of the ship while sailing in will be the Seven Sisters Waterfall. This hanging valley feature results from a sizable river atop the cliffs that is clogged with numerous large boulders that braid the channel thus forcing the water to distribute itself into seven distinct channels before plunging down the face of the cliff, dropping a length of 410 meters or 1,350 feet. It is at its most spectacular flow in late spring and early summer, fed by the melting snow in the higher country above. The water splashes and dashes down the cliff face and when the sun is shining directly above, a beautiful rainbow is created. According to Norse legend, these falls represent seven playful maidens who are flirting with the giant single waterfall across the fjord known as the Suitor. He is also attempting to win their attention, but the primary Norse God is keeping him apart by the depth of the fjord.

GEIRANGER: After passing the Seven Sisters, the ship will round a bend in the fjord and there before you is the village of Geiranger clinging to the shore line. The town with only 300 full time residents is filled with numerous guesthouses, hotels and restaurants, as it is a major gathering place for visitors who are exploring the interior glaciers, lakes and meadows. Geiranger is one of Norway's major tourist destinations. And then entire fjord and surrounding mountain region has been given UNESCO World Heritage Site status.

There is only one small dock in Geiranger and thus most cruise ships will anchor in the fjord and tender guests on shore during their stay. But fortunately the waters are always calm and the distance from the ship to the shore is less than one kilometer. Once on shore, you will either join a motor coach for one of several tours into the high glacial valleys to both enjoy the scenery and the views down upon Geirangerfjorden. Or if you are not comfortable with winding roads and great heights, it is best to simply wander about Geiranger and enjoy the views from lower perspectives.

One of the most exciting and beautiful sights in Geiranger is the cascading river that rushes down from the high glacier to the fjord. There is a massive stairway you can follow from the top end of the fjord that will take you along this thundering torrent all the way up to the high part of Geiranger where you can then follow the main Route 63 back into town, past the Grande Hotel. It is the highlight of walking around in Geiranger.

While on shore, you can dine and sample local Norwegian cuisine. I recommend lunch at the following:

* Brasserie Posten - Located along the Stranda or waterfront, this restaurant is highly rated for its fish soups, fish cakes and fresh vegetables and salads. And of course no Norwegian meal is complete without delicate desserts. But keep in mind that this is a tourist destination and good food is expensive. The restaurant opens at 10:30 AM and remains open until 10 PM.

* Cafe Ole - In the heart of Geiranger's main shopping area and open from 9 AM to 5 PM. I would recommend this cafe for light fare, especially desserts and hot chocolate or excellent coffee.

* Grande Fjord Hotel - Located high above the waterfront on the main road, Route 53. It is one of the larger hotels and impossible to miss. They serve lunch from Noon onward in Restrant Hyskje. Their menu is extensive and of course fish soups, fresh fish, fish cakes and salads are very much a part of what is offered. There are also meat dishes for those wanting to indulge in a heavier meal. And adding to the delicious food is a spectacular view from their picture windows. Breakfast is served from 7:30 to 10 AM, lunch from 1:30 to 5:30 PM and dinner from 7 to 9 PM daily.

* Westeras Gard - Located high above Geiranger on a rather steep walking path that is not recommended for those unable to follow a steep grade. But if you are able to negotiate the path, the view is spectacular. And the food is also excellent, again serving a varied menu. However, roasted goat is considered to be a house specialty. For dessert, they do serve traditional waffles with ice cream and a rich sauce. The restaurant is open from 11 AM to 9 PM Tuesday thru Sunday.

SHOPPING: Geiranger is very much a tourist resort. There are numerous shops selling souvenir arts and crafts, but for the most part the prices are higher than you would find in Bergen or other major cities.

SAILING OUT: If you still have not had enough scenery for one day, you might want to spend time out on deck or in your ship's forward observation lounge during the long sail out through Sognefjorden back to sea. From the time you leave Geiranger it will take about five hours to reach the open sea. And as the day progresses and the sun dips lower on the western horizon, the mountains and shoreline take on a very special glow. It is almost impossible to put into words the majestic aura that is created in the evening light. And few shipboard guests take the chance to enjoy the vistas. I have watched the entire sail out from Geiranger, even missing dinner, just to be able to absorb the changing moods. And clearly I will enjoy it again on future sailings out from Geiranger. It is easy to understand why this is such a popular destination. It is especially beautiful, filled with majestic views and it is in closer proximity to Copenhagen or Oslo to be accessible on shorter cruises than fjords much farther to the north.

THE VILLAGES OF HELLESYLT AND GEIRANGER

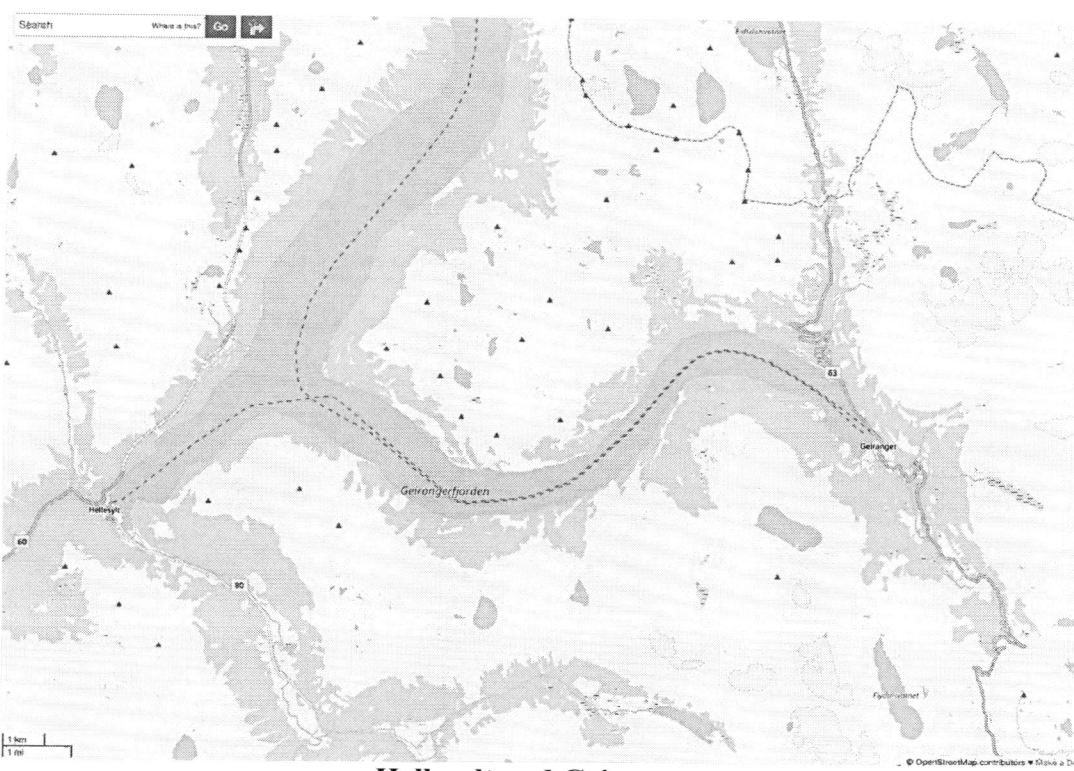

Hellesylt and Geiranger

This map is best viewed directly from OpenStreetMap.com on your personal device where it can be expanded or one specific area can be enlarged. Given the format of this book, it is impossible to display maps with the level of detail you might wish to have while actually out exploring the city. But the OpenStreetMap maps used directly are the tool I always rely upon.

THE CENTER OF GEIRANGER

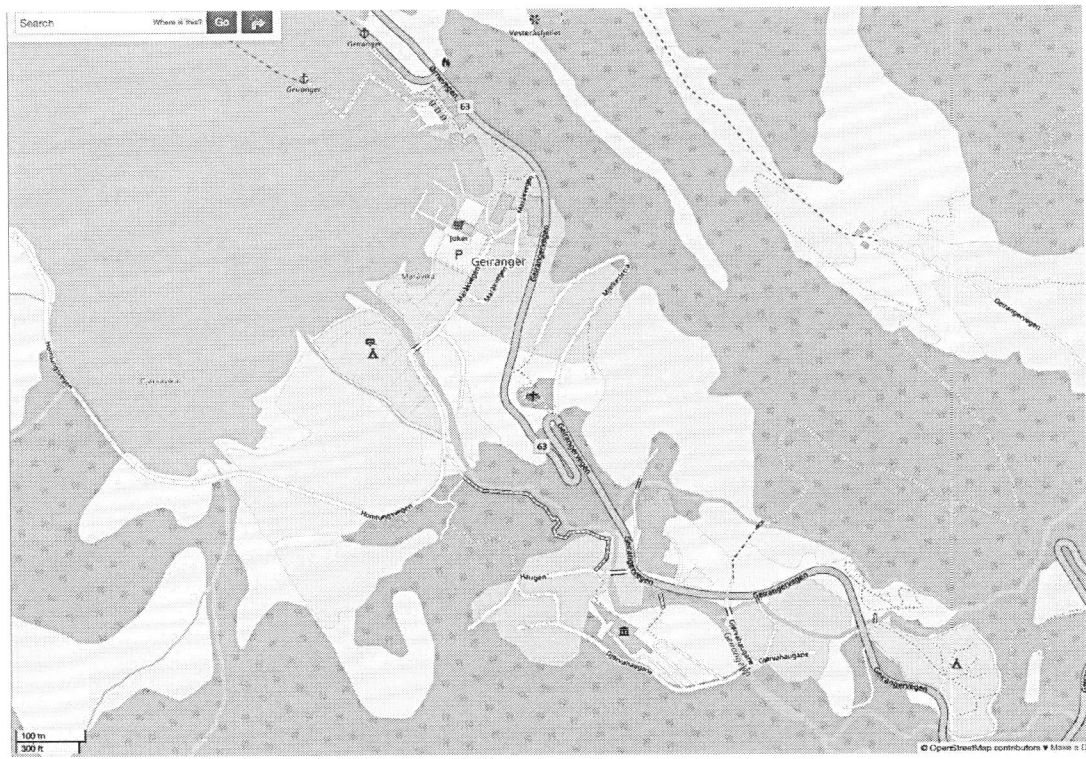

The village of Geiranger

This map is best viewed directly from OpenStreetMap.com on your personal device where it can be expanded or one specific area can be enlarged. Given the format of this book, it is impossible to display maps with the level of detail you might wish to have while actually out exploring the city. But the OpenStreetMap maps used directly are the tool I always rely upon.

Entering Storfjorden in the early morning

Entering Næyorfjorden

Approaching Hellesyilt

The village of Hellesylt and its thundering waterfall

The meeting of Storfjorden and Geirangerfjorden

The Seven Sisters Waterfall in Geirangerfjorden

A closer view of the Seven Sisters Waterfall

Looking down at Geiranger

The village of Geiranger from the plateau above

The beauty of the whitewater Geiranger River

At the top of the Geiranger River where it plunges over a cliff

High above Geiranger on the way to the glaciers

Still higher above Geiranger en route to the glacier

A spectacular view down to Geirangerfjorden

High up above timberline

The glacial lake high above Geiranger

Up in glacier country where snow never melts completely

The high mountain roads are not for the faint of heart

Storfjorden in the late evening while sailing out toward the sea

Approaching the sea from Storfjorden at 11 PM

KRISTIANSUND

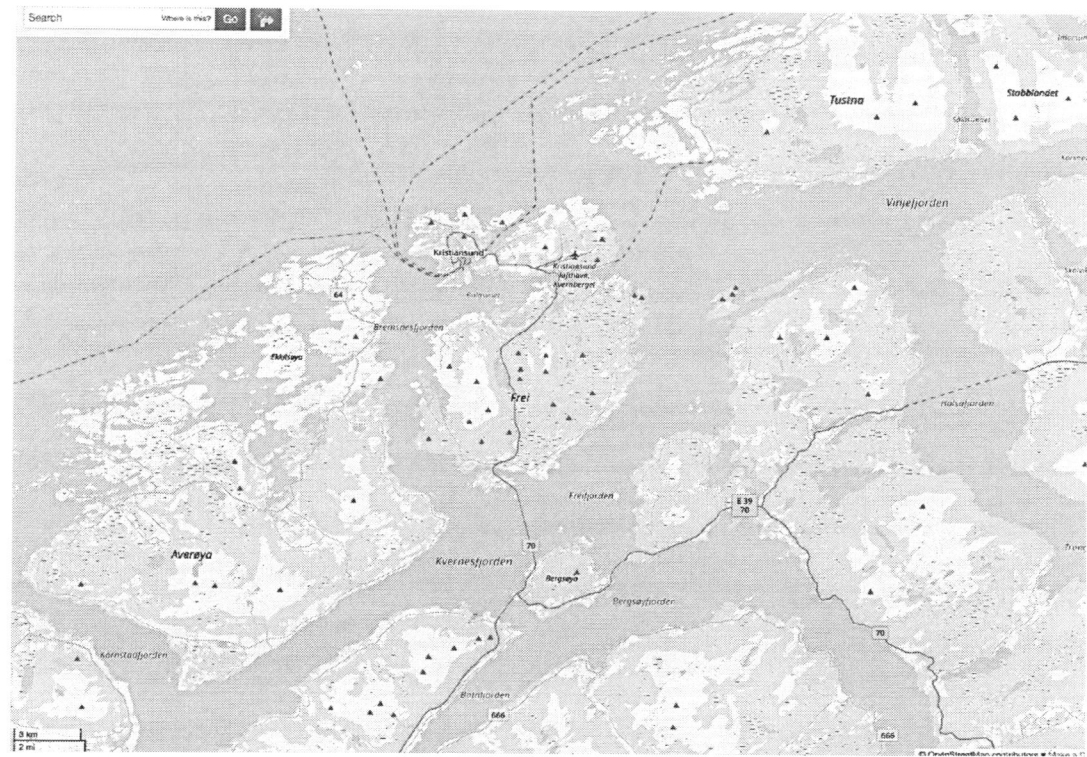

The coastal islands around Kristiansund (© OpenStreetMap contributors)

Kristiansund is the major city and administrative center in the Nordmøe region just north of Storfjorden. Not all cruise ships make a stop at this city whose history celebrates the one time importance of cod fishing. Today Kristiansund is very much a blue-collar city that supports various maintenance projects out on the North Sea oil drilling platforms. With a population of around 20,000, it is a substantial community, but one that many cruise passengers do not find as enjoyable because most of its historic architecture perished during World War II.

THE GEOGRAPHIC SETTING: Kristiansund is a city by the sea, yet it turns its back to the harsh North Sea and faces inward, clustered on four islands around a sheltered central harbor. The city is quite densely populated, as its 20,000 residents occupy only 7.9 square kilometers, thus making it one of the country's most concentrated cities. Yet you will not feel a sense of crowding because of the fact that the city climbs steep hillsides on all four of its islands and the high ground is topped off by beautiful woodland. Facing out to sea on the backside of the northern and western islands, the land shows its rugged granite base, offering no beaches or safe anchorage. And in winter, it can be lashed by strong wind and surf.

Notwithstanding its island location, its proximity to the mainland has enabled Kristiansund to be connected by bridges and thus it does not quite feel like it is isolated from the rest of the nation. And it is also connected to a string of islands on which there are small fishing villages by a series of undersea tunnels and bridges known as the Great Atlantic Road. Apart from its very scenic potential and it being an architectural wonder, it is part of a very extensive system of roads that connect many of the near offshore islands to the mainland all along the Norwegian coast. The country has invested heavily in its infrastructure.

Despite its great oil wealth, Norway uses only monies raised through taxation for its superb infrastructure development. The entire earnings from the oil fields is placed in a superbly managed national pension fund. With its small population, everyone is able to retire and receive an annual pension essentially equal to their highest period of earning plus full medical coverage. The Norwegian people have the greatest degree of financial security of any nation in the world. Even with today's lower oil prices, Norway's pension fund continues to grow because of the high degree of management of the investment.

Kristiansund's climate is that of a temperate marine regime. Summers are relatively cool and sunny days are interspersed with cloudy periods that bring rain showers. When visiting in the summer, it is rather hit or miss as to having a bright sunny day. Being closer to the Arctic Circle, Kristiansund has long winter nights with very short days, but its snowfall accumulation is far less than cities that are sheltered from the sea by way of being on the inner channels or deep into the fjords. But temperatures are still cold, hovering around the freezing mark. Winter days can be quite blustery and bone chilling.

THE FASCINATING HISTORY: To appreciate your visit to Kristiansund it is important to have some understanding of the city's history. The first thing that will strike you when sailing into the harbor is the lack of a sense of history in its architecture. And this is part of the overall story of the city.

The Norwegian coast has a long history of settlement. There is archaeological evidence of pre Viking tribes having moved north along the edges of the retreating glacial ice as far back as 10,000 years ago. With the melt water mixing with seawater, high nutrient plankton provided a base for a rich and diverse marine population of shellfish and fish, and this encouraged human settlement along the coast.

Although during Viking times there were various battles fought in the immediate area, Kristiansund was never known to have been settled by the Norse warrior tribes.

During the Middle Ages, as Christianity was extending into Norway and the Norse tribes were settling down and developing more of a sedentary life, only the small island of Grip, off the coast from Kristiansund, saw any development as a fishing port. And it is assumed that the fishermen would have exploited the waters around what is now Kristiansund. An early Christian stave church is believed to have been built in 1470 in the village of Grip. The island continues to be inhabited to the present day, and it is connected during the summer by ferry to Kristiansund, a journey of approximately 30-minutes. But Grip does face the full fury of North Sea storms and the island has been swamped many times.

Kristiansund only dates to the mid 1600's, when the first fishermen began to settle here. By the late 1600's, there was sufficient settlement based upon fishing and lumber to warrant the establishment of a government customs outpost. But it was in the waning years of the 17th century that Kristiansund's future was determined. Thanks to the introduction of the technique for drying cod, then a plentiful and bountiful species, exploitation began. And with a ready market in countries such as Portugal and Spain, Kristiansund became one of the most important fishing ports along the Norwegian coast. Known in the Norwegian language as "klippfisk," salted and dried cod was a basic staple to feed the hungry populations of the Iberian Peninsula and other parts of the western Mediterranean.

The importance of klippfisk is what put Kristiansund on the map, the town being given a city charter in 1742. The growth of Kristiansund was facilitated by the abundance of timber, and apart from the main church and the 19th century concert hall, the majority of buildings consisted of wood siding. There were occasional outbreaks of fire, but it was not until World War II and the Nazi occupation of Norway that Kristiansund would see a major conflagration. To exhort submission prior to occupying the port for military purposes, the German air force firebombed Kristiansund, destroying most of the community. Only the stone buildings survived to the present day. This is why Kristiansund lacks a distinctive architecture, as the majority of the city is of post-World War II origin.

One of the most tragic moments of the Nazi occupation of the city was the rounding up of 18 Jewish citizens that ranged in age from five up into the 70's. They were shipped off to one of the concentration/death camps and nobody survived to return to Kristiansund. There is a small memorial in the park just up the hill from the city center and opposite the modern city church.

With the discovery of oil in the North Sea, Kristiansund became one of the major service centers for the oil drilling and pumping platforms just over the horizon out at sea. The city also is home to the families of many of the oil workers who commute between the city and the platforms, living out at sea for periods of time before returning to the city. This has brought new life to Kristiansund since cod fishing has been greatly diminished by the declining numbers of fish and strict quotas as to their harvesting.

Tourism plays a small role in the city's economy because it is not located in one of the most scenic of areas, and it is not easy to reach in contrast to the many fjords where there is a strong tourist focus. Few cruise ships call in at Kristiansund, but for those that do, the people are quite welcoming.

WHAT TO SEE AND DO: Much will depend upon your cruise line with regard to tours outside of Kristiansund. Some of the smaller more upmarket cruise lines offer a tour by motor coach along the Great Ocean Road, which can be quite spectacular on a nice sunny day. Some cruise lines offer more adventure oriented kayaking or sailing tours, and on occasion I have seen a tour to the historic island of Grip.

The most commonly offered tour is a four-hour guided tour by motor coach around the city of Kristiansund with a visit to the klippfisk museum where you learn the history of cod fishing, salting and drying and its impact upon the growth of the city. But many will choose to simply walk the community, and if that is your choice, here are the major highlights:

* Bautean - This is the high hill where the canon is fired to welcome a cruise ship into port. It is a bit of a climb, but well worth the imposing view of the city and out to the surrounding islands. You can reach it by walking across the high bridge to Innlandet Island or by taking

the ferryboat and getting off at the first stop. There are no given hours, but the trail has no lighting and if visiting in the spring or fall one should never walk the route after dark.

* Holocaust Memorial - Just down the hill from the church about one full block in the park is the memorial, which is somewhat hidden away. It is a very poignant reminder of the Holocaust and its impact upon Kristiansund. The memorial sits in the park and thus is always open to visitors.

* Kirkelandet Kirke - This ultra-modern new church has replaced the old stone church across the harbor as the main Lutheran church for the city. It has beautiful stained glass windows and is worth a short visit. The church is open to visitors, but there may be special services when tourists are not permitted. No actual visitation hours are posted.

* Mellemværftet Shipbuilding Museum - Located down a steep hill from the main strand that runs along the harbor. This rather small museum is really for those who have a special interest in how the old fishing vessels were built back in the time period when Kristiansund was at the height of its cod fishing period. It is open daily from Noon to 5 PM, and very welcoming especially when a cruise ship is in port.

* Nordlandet Kirke - On the Nordlandet Island, which is the second ferry stop, you can see this old stone church up close. It is built of stone, but only dates back to 1914, and is one of the few buildings to survive the bombing of World War II. No specific visiting hours are posted, so you may find the church closed. Usually the doors are open on days when a ship is in port.

* Norwegian Klippfisk Museum - This is a major feature on the ship sponsored tour, but if you want to go on your own, you will need to take a taxi as it is too far to walk. You can take the ferryboat, getting off at the final stop, but it is a steep walk up to the museum. The guided tour is quite fascinating and it surprises you how much there is to learn. The museum is open from Noon to 5 PM daily.

* Sundbaten - This yellow ferryboat that you will see at the World War II monument with the surrounding Norwegian flags is one quick way to spend time visiting all of the islands that make up the city. It travels in a counterclockwise direction, so you can either stay on for the entire ride or get off and catch some of the recommended sights. The ferry runs quite often and has its schedule posted.

* Varden Tower - This is the best way to get a visual overview of the city. It is a short distance from the city center, but it is not well marked. Stop at the local tourist office in the city center to ask specific directions. Essentially you start at the new church on the hill above the city center, follow the main street, which is Langveien for one long block to Vuggaveien and turn left, the right at the first cross street, which is Hagbart Brinchmanns vei and you will see the path to the tower on your left. The tower has a button at the door and when pressed, it triggers an automatic opener. No specific hours are posted, but it is generally open when ships are in port.

DINING OUT: Kristiansund has numerous restaurants, but you must remember that this is a blue collar community of fishermen and oil workers So do not expect gourmet quality or ambiance. I have eaten lunch in Kristiansund numerous times over the years, and these are my recommendations:

* Bryggekanten Brasserie - Located along the waterfront near to where cruise ships dock. It has a good reputation for quality cuisine and service. And it has great views of the harbor. Open from 11:30 AM to 10:30 PM, you will not go wrong dining here. They offer a variety of seafood and meat dishes, including burgers to satisfy those from North America.

Dodeladen Cafe og Kultursted - On the waterfront in the center of town very close to where cruise ships dock at Skippergata # 1a, this is a popular restaurant with a large outdoor deck overlooking the harbor. Again traditionally prepared seafood dishes dominate the menu, including the traditional baccalao, which had made Kristiansund famous. The restaurant is open Tuesday thru Thursday from 2 to 11 PM, Friday and Saturday from 2 Pm to Midnight and Sunday from 1 PM to Midnight.

* Nordmorskafeen Homemade Food - Located along the waterfront at Fosnagata #3 upstairs, and open from 9 AM to 6 PM, this is my favorite place for traditional, well-prepared Norwegian dishes. It is not fancy, and you order at the counter and then select your beverage and dessert. When the main course is ready, it is brought to your table. The staff is very friendly and will make substitutions to accommodate your tastes. Their menu is small, but changes daily. I have never had a bad lunch here.

* Sjøstjerna - Located in the city center on Skolegata. It is open from Noon to Midnight and serves genuine Norwegian cuisine, primarily specializing in fresh fish and seafood. But the food and service are good, and the atmosphere is typical of the cozy restaurants of the city. One of the specialties is bacalao, which is the Portuguese way of reconstituting dried and salted cod. It is very good and now accepted as a local delicacy. If fiskeboller are on the menu, it is my favorite. It is made from chopped fish that is formed into what would be like meatballs and then poached in a fish broth.

* Smia Fish Restauant - Located along the downtown waterfront at Fosnagata #30b, this is a very traditional seafood restaurant in which authenticity rules. If you want to experience the best of Norwegian seafood preparation while in Kristiansund, this is the restaurant to try. It is open Monday thru Saturday 11 AM to 10 PM and on Sunday from 2 to 6 PM.
If you are simply in the mood for dessert, the shopping mall across the street from where the ship docks has a very good pastry counter on the second floor. They offer sandwiches and pastries with coffee or tea, and it can sometimes be just the light snack you are looking for.

SHOPPING: There are few shops that offer souvenirs or hand crafted items, as the tourist market is small. Opposite where the ship docks is the city's main indoor shopping arcade with dozens of shops on two levels. This mall serves local needs, but is interesting to visit. Across from the mall in the parking lot there are often vendors selling fresh fish and berries along with various pastries.

FINAL WORDS: Many of my fellow passengers have asked why the ship bothered to stop in Kristiansund, as they found it less interesting than other ports. But these people clearly had either not read up on the history of the town or attended my presentation. Kristiansund is not one of the more illustrious communities on the itinerary, but it is definitely interesting in giving you a look at a hard working blue-collar Norwegian coastal town.

MAPS OF KRISTIANSUND

THE MAIN ISLANDS OF KRISTIANSUND

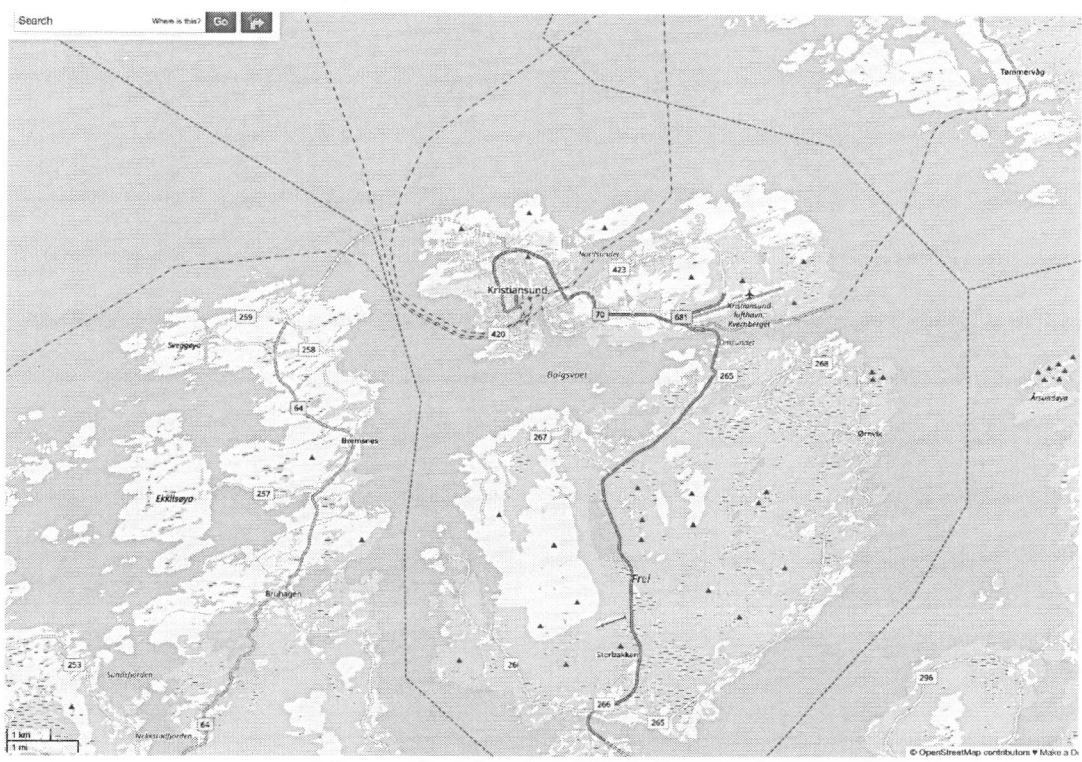

The main islands of Kristiansund

This map is best viewed directly from OpenStreetMap.com on your personal device where it can be expanded or one specific area can be enlarged. Given the format of this book, it is impossible to display maps with the level of detail you might wish to have while actually out exploring the city. But the OpenStreetMap maps used directly are the tool I always rely upon.

THE CITY OF KRISTIANSUND

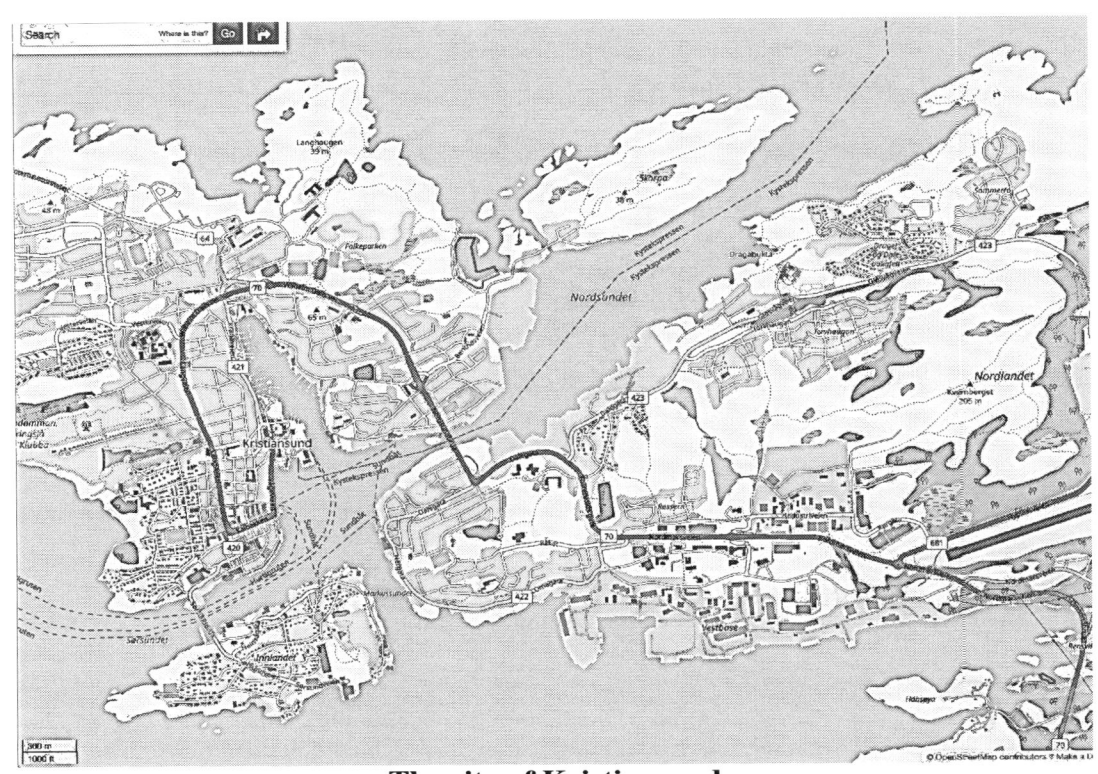

The city of Kristiansund

This map is best viewed directly from OpenStreetMap.com on your personal device where it can be expanded or one specific area can be enlarged. Given the format of this book, it is impossible to display maps with the level of detail you might wish to have while actually out exploring the city. But the OpenStreetMap maps used directly are the tool I always rely upon.

THE CENTER OF KRISTIANSUND

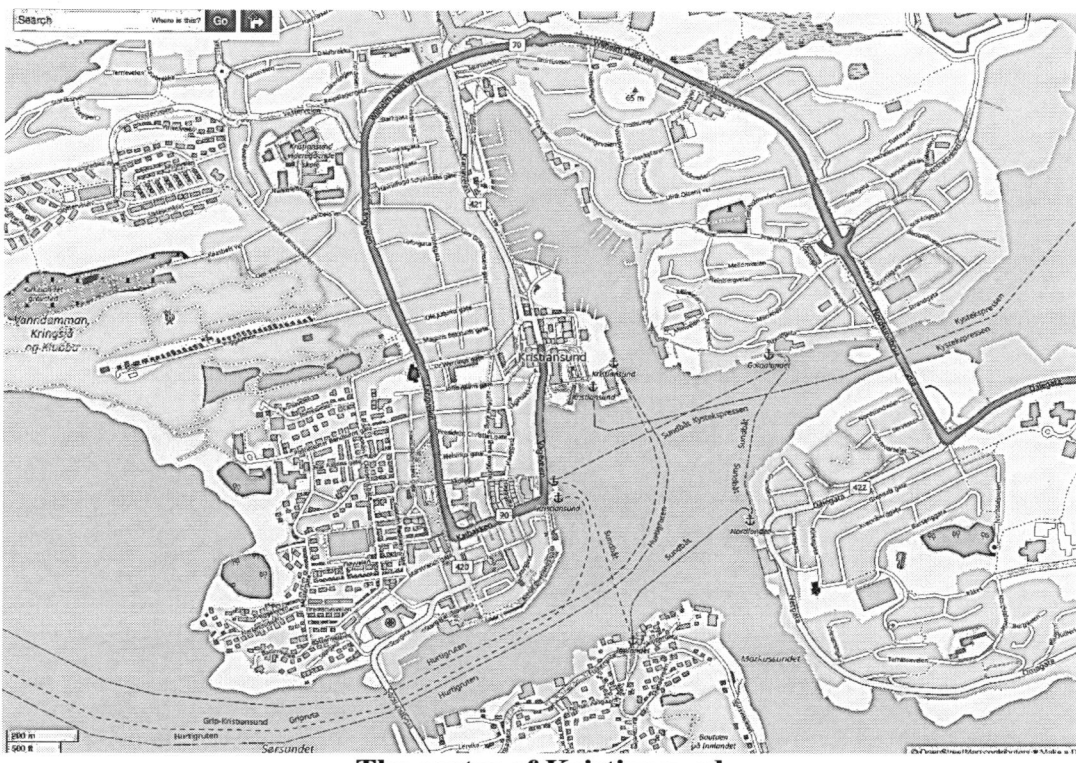

The center of Kristiansund

This map is best viewed directly from OpenStreetMap.com on your personal device where it can be expanded or one specific area can be enlarged. Given the format of this book, it is impossible to display maps with the level of detail you might wish to have while actually out exploring the city. But the OpenStreetMap maps used directly are the tool I always rely upon.

The outer suburbs of Kristiansund on Innlandet Island

Docking in the town center of Kristiansund

The main waterfront strand seen from onboard ship

One of the oil platform service vessels docked in the city center

On the waterfront in the city center with its war monument

Flower beds in the heart of Kristiansund

Fresh cut flowers for indoor enjoyment during the brief summer

The inscriptions on the Kristiansund Holocaust Memorial showing the names and ages of the victims

The war memorial to the 18 Kristiansund Jews who were sent off to the Nazi death camps during World War II

Summer is strawberry season in Kristiansund

The old stone church survived the Nazi bombings in WWII

Festival Hall also survived the bombings of WWII

ABOUT THE AUTHOR

Dr. Lew Deitch

I am a semi-retired professor of geography with over 46 years of teaching experience. During my distinguished career, I directed the Honors Program at Northern Arizona University and developed many programs relating to the study of contemporary world affairs. I am an honors graduate of The University of California, Los Angeles, earned my Master of Arts at The University of Arizona and completed my doctorate in geography at The University of New England in Australia. I am a globetrotter, having visited 92 countries on all continents except Antarctica. My primary focus is upon human landscapes, especially such topics as local architecture, foods, clothing and folk music. I am also a student of world politics and conflict.

I enjoy being in front of an audience, and have spoken to thousands of people at civic and professional organizations. I have been lecturing on board ships for Silversea Cruises since 2008. I love to introduce people to exciting new places both by means of presenting vividly illustrated talks and through serving as a tour consultant for ports of call. I am also an avid writer, and for years I have written my own text books used in my university classes. Now I have turned my attention to writing travel companions, books that will introduce you to the country you are visiting, but not serving as a touring book like the major guides you find in all of the bookstores.

I also love languages, and my skills include a conversational knowledge of German, Russian and Spanish.

I was raised in California, have lived in Canada and Australia. Arizona has been his permanent home since 1974. One exciting aspect of my life was the ten-year period, during which I volunteered my time as an Arizona Highway Patrol reserve trooper, working out on the streets and highways and also developing new safety and enforcement programs for use statewide. I presently live just outside of Phoenix in the beautiful resort city of Scottsdale and still offer a few courses for the local community colleges when I am at home.

I would like to extend an invitation for you to join me on one of the Silversea cruise segments when I am on board presenting my destination talks. You would find it to be a wonderful experience, especially after having read my book on this area, or on the others I have written about.

FOR MORE INFORMATION REGARDING TRAVELING ON BOARD WHEN I AM THE SPEAKER, CONTACT, WESTSIDE INTERNATIONAL TRAVEL, THE TRAVEL AGENCY I USE FOR ALL MY TRAVELS AT:
www.westsideintltravel.com

TO CONTACT ME, PLEASE CHECK OUT MY WEB PAGE FOR MORE INFORMATION AT:
http://www.doctorlew.com

Printed in Great Britain
by Amazon